ART

The Church's Response

RICK SORENSON

The Lanyap Life Books

ISBN: 9798985927764 (Paperback)
ISBN: 9798985927771 (Ebook)

Library of Congress Control Number: 2023931595

Front Cover Art: Paintings
Top painting, "Landscape" 1993, by Rick Sorenson
Bottom painting, "Landscape: Two Hills" 1993, by Rick Sorenson

The Lanyap Life Books
1116 Vista Avenue #353
Boise, Idaho 83705

www.thelanyaplife.com/books

ACKNOWLEDGMENTS

In 2013, I was in Milwaukee, Wisconsin, attending a Southern Graphics Council International (SGCI) printmakers conference. A long-time friend from the SGCI conferences, Tom Conrad, of Conrad Press, said, "Let's get some coffee." We went to a coffee shop to catch up, while his wife, Dorthy, watched their vendor's booth. During our catching up, Tom told me, "You should write a book on Art to Christians."

On the way home from the conference, Tom's words resonated in my mind. Some of this book's outline began to form at this time. I am grateful for Tom and Dorthy Conrad's friendship. They are great examples of Christians involved in the artworld.

I want to thank the people who read my manuscript at various stages through the years and gave me their feedback. I considered all their suggestions. This book is better because of them. So, thank you Colleen Mathisen, Phillip Wyns, Anthony Williams, Fred Kropp, and Brian Parsons.

I talked through many spiritual and psychological concepts with my Dad, Dick Sorenson, as I wrote this book. As a pastor and therapist, he helped me to better understand how the Hebrew and Greek words relay their concepts. Our discussions on how ideas form in the brain gave clarity to how I finally came to describe the process.

Both my parents, Dick and Donna Sorenson, encouraged me to pursue the path that God led me through in the arts. They never saw creative endeavors as bad. Because of their support, I was free to follow God wherever He led.

A special thank you goes to Strachelle Wyns. She edited my manuscript with grace and fortitude. Her challenges for clarity I took to heart. She did not take everything at face value, but required me to help her understand, thereby making it understandable for the reader. I appreciate her maturity in Christ, which enabled her to complete several ideas when I stopped just short.

Tami Gaupp, of The Lanyap Life Books, amiably said yes to publishing my manuscript. She was enthusiastic in her support of the endeavor. And being my little sister helped.

And a big, big thank you to my wife, Jesika Sorenson. She was great at pointing out holes in the manuscript. I love her more today than when we married.

I can say the Holy Spirit was with me throughout the process of writing this book, by clarifying ideas and thoughts, the many, many insights I received from Scripture, bringing books on a topic at the time I needed to consider the ideas and giving me the enabling power to do what He put on my heart. I am so grateful to the Lord for His mercy to me.

CONTENTS

INTRODUCTION

God's Spirit is stirring this generation to the arts.

I wrote this book, *ART: The Church's Response*, as a help toward perceiving the arts through a biblical perspective. God is releasing creativity in greater ways in our era. Therefore, we cannot keep our eyes closed. Let us open ourselves to cooperate with God as the Holy Spirit ignites people's creative expressions. Throughout this book, we will explore how the Bible addresses many issues related to creativity and the arts.

Paradoxically, Christians are not generally interested in the arts—the primary outlets of our God-given creativity. Some people may ask, "Why does it matter? Art is frivolous when compared to the truly significant issues." This pious response sounds right but is fabricated on a lie. The foremost reason creativity should be judged worthy of attention, is that God is first revealed as Creator. We are made in God's image, so we also are creators. The arts are one area of expression among many where we use creativity. Society meaningfully relates with our world through its engagements through the arts.

For many of us, the enemy of God shamed us from our creativity, and this is the foundation for the belief, "we are not creative". This perverse notion shaped our view towards the arts, even how we live life. We extended our "not-creative" perspective beyond the personal, to an overall rejection of various creative categories. Despite our denials, God ingrained a creative nature in us. The reason we should care about the arts, even if we are not an artist creating, is because we have God's creativity. Satan and his devils made a targeted effort to veil and distort our thoughts towards creativity; to conquer their lies, we must replace them with God's Truth. Even if many Christians may not overcome the indoctrination about their creativity, we need not remain trapped by the enemy's lie but can be free through the blood of Jesus. Let us stop propagating falsehoods and share how God set creativity in each person, waiting for release and development. Our very nature empowers us to bring ideas to reality and to enjoy the products of our and others' imagination. Everything around us originated in someone's imagination.

SCHAEFFER/ROOKMAAKER'S FOUNDATION

Over the centuries, people involved with the arts sought to understand creativity's workings. Sometimes the theorizing lined up with the Bible, and other times the enemy injected ideas to confuse the issues.

In the 1960s, 70s, and 80s, Francis Schaeffer and H. R. Rookmaaker showed Christians that art is not contrary to Scripture. Since then, the Church has been more accepting of the arts. I am grateful to them. Through the years, I read many Christian writings on art reiterating points set forth by Schaeffer and Rookmaaker. It seems our understanding has not grown beyond the reiterated points.

I hope this book extends beyond the foundation they laid, even to the point we may "leave the elementary doctrine of Christ and go on to maturity, not laying again a foundation of repentance from dead works and of faith towards God" (Hebrews 6:1). I will not restate Schaeffer and Rookmaaker's justification for the arts. If you need further explanation, I recommend Schaefer's book, *Art and the Bible* (1973) and Rookmaaker's book, *The Creative Gift: Essays on Art and the Creative Life* (1981).

BACKGROUND

Let me share some background, confirming that I can address many issues connected to creativity and the arts. As a preacher's kid, I am familiar with the things that go on in churches, both good and bad. Concerning art interest, I learned to draw in 7th, 8th, and 9th grades; attended an art college, where I graduated with a drawing and painting degree, and years later, was listed in a Who's Who of the World (2000). I am familiar with the art world and the Christian world, including the strengths and weaknesses of both. If the Church is to extend Christ's influence with creative people, even upon the arts themselves, we must familiarize ourselves with the strengths and weaknesses of creative people.

THE MINISTRY OF RECONCILIATION

Those coming from the opinion "art is unimportant for existence" may reason, "Why should we apply ourselves towards the arts, as there are more crucial areas of life?"

Reviewing the epochs of human history, we notice a general habit: at the end of a hard day of tending fields and animals, a family or a clan would gather to unwind while carving sticks, singing songs, telling stories, playing an instrument, etc. The time and energy we exert in any creative endeavor takes us out of our usual lethargy, reconnecting us to ourselves and to each other. Our life is more than survival. Let me emphasize this point: creative endeavors restore and realign us to God's creative image.

When we take on God's view of creating, creativity, and creation, both for ourselves and towards others, we reconcile creativity to God's purpose. For this reason, we have "the ministry of reconciliation."

Therefore, if anyone is in Christ, he is a new creation. The old has passed away; behold, the new has come. All this is from God, who through Christ reconciled us to himself and gave us the ministry of reconciliation; that is, in Christ God was reconciling the world to himself, not counting their trespasses against them, and entrusting to us the message of reconciliation.

2 Corinthians 5:17-19

An excellent measure for aligning to God's perspective is to view the arts as a mission field. Just as a missionary prepares to go to a people group or country and then is sent out by the Church, so we prepare ourselves for the people group called Artists in the *Land of The Arts,* to bring God's light to their territory. But the Church as a whole, has largely rejected this people group, consigning them to the dark. Christians expected artists to adjust themselves to pious ways, which they in turn rejected. From my observations, the reason the Peoples of *The Arts* refuse the Christians' proposal to change themselves to religious niceties is because the offer is without love, showing little desire to extend the ministry of reconciliation to the *Land of the Arts.*

THE CURRENT APPROACH

Most Christians regard art as a tool for communication. We assume that an idea's transmission is vital. When a work spreads a message we condemn, we judge art a problem. Christians try to solve art's dilemma by guaranteeing the message is "correct".

There are some traditional messages proclaimed by the Church, such as: Christians should only be about God and God's Glory. To this end, we must guarantee each person's sinfulness is known and therefore declare the proper behavior for our culture, such as ensuring music is not too fast nor mesmerizing, which would compel us to dance and carouse with the opposite sex. Life is not a party. You can have fun, but not *too* much fun.

Is this point of view accurate? This take on the "Christian Perspective" is a Sacred versus Secular outlook that appraises the "cause and effect" of a work. The work causes a response in the viewer, and we, as Christians, judge its presumed effect. When we evaluate works through a Sacred/Secular lens, we judge its perceived morality.

What result has the Sacred/Secular morality achieved with the People of the *Land of the Arts*? We pushed people away from Christ. Our present society, its culture, and the culture of the arts are the result.

ART DEFINED

If we are to carry out the ministry of reconciliation towards creativity and the Peoples in the *Land of the Arts*, we must prepare ourselves to go. Therefore, let us try to define with clarity what art is about. People may be able to recognize art but then struggle to define it. Art is not restricted to a visual image, though this is the meaning most people associate. We articulate our human-ness through Dance, Drama, Music, Visual, Writing, and any other creative form. Art expresses what we feel, think, believe, and wish, even if it's not pretty. Works of art may touch us deeply, and provoke strong emotions or opinions, even when our judgments may not align with the works. To state the point clearly: art communicates our human-ness. Art is expression, but not every expression is art. There is a distinction. A reading of Chapter 3, entitled "Testing Works," will assist the reader to better distinguish the difference.

MORALITY'S LENS

Most Christians regard the arts through a moral lens, being concerned with its communications. Art has a relatively small percentage of immoral subjects. But, for the sake of argument, let us assign twenty percent of all art as immoral. What happens with the other eighty percent? We associate the majority with the condemned twenty percent. Mass condemnation does not convert artists to Christ. So, in what manner should we consider the arts?

Theologian, Francis Schaeffer proposed a way to test art: Technical Excellence, Validity, Intellectual Content, and Integration of Content and Vehicle (the art medium). [1] Nowhere did Francis Schaeffer specify that content should be the "right kind." We have added to Schaeffer's criteria, inspecting works through an assumed rightness or wrongness.

FUTILE THINKING

What happens if we apply the moral judgment used for others to ourselves? Will our own communication hold up and meet the Scriptural standard, especially if we include any accusations, condemnations, and gossiping that seem to occur throughout churches, or anything we put on social media? If God's love does not flow through us, our everyday communication will be as the Apostle Paul described: futile in their thinking and their foolish hearts were darkened (Romans 1:21). Without God's love, we cannot trust our reasoning, because we misperceive situations and pass on thoughts and intents devoid of God's light. Beyond misperceiving, when we do not operate through God's love, our hearts will not display God's righteousness, or right-ness, and we will express futile thoughts from our natural "darkened heart." The Apostle Paul tells us the result of the "dark heart" condition.

And since they did not see fit to acknowledge God, God gave them up to a debased mind, to do what ought not to be done. They were filled with all manner of unrighteousness, evil, covetousness, malice. They are full of envy, murder, strife, deceit, maliciousness. They are gossips, slanderers, haters of God, insolent, haughty, boastful, inventors of evil, disobedient to parents, foolish, faithless, heartless, ruthless. Though they knew God's righteous decree that those who practice such things deserve to die, they not only do them, but give approval to those who practice them.

Romans 1:28-32

Most Christians view these verses as applying to non-Christians and our overall society. While this is the context of the passage and the normal interpretation, I see it *also* applies to everyone whose judgments are futile, including those in the Church, as Paul shows a few verses down in Romans 2:1-6. I will highlight verse 1 and finish out Paul's thought from verse 1 with his statement in verse twenty-four.

Therefore, you have no excuse, O man, every one of you who judges. For in passing judgment on another you condemn yourself, because you, the judge, practice the same things.

Romans 2:1

For as it is written, "The name of God is blasphemed among the Gentiles because of you."

Romans 2:24

All of us hold to some foolish beliefs because society indoctrinated us in soulish reasoning. But we can get beyond our futile judgments. Jesus took our place at the cross. Now we reckon ourselves dead to sin and may let go of our "dark heart." We are a new person, with a new heart because of Christ's resurrection, and God adopted us into his family as sons and daughters. We put off the old ways of reasoning and put on the mind of Christ.

When we operate from a "dark heart" condition, we judge. Let us remember that God's loving-kindness and mercy are greater than our conclusions and verdicts. Our judgments present to others a false view of God because a divine sentence has not yet occurred but mercy through Christ.

Many people reading this may wonder, "But what does all this have to do with art?" I am glad you asked. I will illustrate a way our judgments have pushed artists away from Christ.

MY EXPERIENCE

When I attended art school, I met many people who had once been open to God, until a Christian person or two offended them. I heard several students' experiences; each student conveyed the manner Christians' religious piety condemned their pursuit towards artistic expressions. For many of the students, the sacred/secular censure they encountered left unanswered the questions about life and eternity, and they rejected anything the offending Christian espoused and stood for, including Jesus. Afterwards, they explored other areas for their answers: other religions, magic/witchcraft, philosophy, politics, and art.

Christians also condemned me in the same manner as the other students in art school. Let me recount my incident. I attended art school full time, paying for it myself, worked two part-time jobs, and was active in my church, which was an hour drive away. My time was precious; I often gave up sleep to meet people and participate in events. For one of my jobs, I worked as an overnight security guard. I went to a small home group for a Bible study on Tuesday nights before working the security job. The home group met in a couple's home about 30-40 minutes from where I lived. To meet a school drawing requirement, I drew the coffee table arrangement in my sketchbook during the small group and still joined the discussions more than most people in the group.

After two years of attending the small group, one night a church leader looked through my sketchbook. Everyone is curious about what is in an artist's sketchbook. Mine contained, along with the drawings of coffee table arrangements, male and female nude figure studies, from the times I used the sketchbook in my figure drawing class. As the leader looked through my sketchbook and noticed the figure studies, they questioned whether I was really a Christian. How could I be a Christian and go to art school? After the person viewed my sketchbook, I endured most of an hour interrogation, during which they questioned my commitment to Christ, until I needed to leave for work. I suffered through two more incidents of attack, after which I continued to show up at the small group Bible study with the person who publicly passed judgment on me. Additionally, I continued to see this person at church. Because of their denouncements, and actions, they severed the relationship I had with their family.

A Christian leader passed judgment over me from their assumptions, then issued sentence. This person did not characterize Christ. They unwittingly repeated the accusing and condemning words of God's enemy, which were not of life but death.

I had to forgive that individual many times for their judgments and condemnation. Then I applied Romans 8:1-2 to my life: "There is therefore now no condemnation for those who are in Christ Jesus. For the law of the Spirit of life has set you free in Christ Jesus from the law of sin and death." I nailed on the cross and released the betrayal, hurt, anger, offense, and condemnation so I could embrace the law of the Spirit of life.

My experience is illustrative of the way Christians often represent Jesus to the People in the *Land of the Arts*. The Church denounced the arts a long time ago, and removed itself from engaging in art's pursuits, which left the arts to drift anywhere. Over time, churchy deliberations doubted the arts came from God. The Church's withdrawal from the arts and its related areas of culture allowed society to get caught up with the things floating in the general current, and the result is today's cultural philosophy. Despite this, God has not abandoned us. Through the centuries, God brought along many Christians into artistic endeavors and influence. Today, God uses us.

TOPICS IN THIS BOOK

As you read this book, remember, God is awakening Christians to the arts! The enemy attempts to keep everyone from plugging into their God-given creativity, injecting wrong perceptions towards the arts through societal indoctrination. This book will challenge our presumptions so that we may change whatever does not hold true to the biblical perspective on creativity. The way I set about testing our views towards art is to examine many Bible verses that touch on various issues pertaining to art, and I even investigate the Hebrew and Greek words used in Scripture. I do not assume the arts are separate from life. Creativity weaves and interconnects through out our life. Therefore, I address various areas of relevance: creating, appraising, some abstract issues, and challenge our assumptions about Christian living which influence our notions of art. I wrote this book from a maker's perspective *and* an audience's outlook, sometimes switching from one point of view to the other. We need both views to understand God's gift of creativity. This is not a book of theory but always has in mind the ministry of reconciliation, in a personal sense of letting go the lies we assumed true, and for encouraging others because God put His image inside them. Also, I am *not* relaying everything the Bible has to say about creativity and the arts, but have aimed to address its essential perspective.

———

The topical areas covered in this book:

Chapter 1. In the Beginning
We start with Genesis, looking at God creating. We examine some barriers to creating and the creative process itself. We also clarify messy words: creativity, imagination, and inspiration.

Chapter 2. What is a Work?

How does Scripture talk about works?

Chapter 3. Testing Works

In what manner do we evaluate people's works?

Chapter 4. Kingdom Thinking with Art

What is Kingdom of God thinking, as applied to the arts?

Chapter 5. Audience

Who do we make works for?

Chapter 6. Significant Form

What is significant form?

Chapter 7. The Purpose of It All

How do we use our gifts?

———

Through your gifts, follow the Holy Spirit's leading. Enjoy your skills and abilities, and take pleasure in your works, for that is a gift of God (Ecclesiastes 3:13).

The Christian public often stays behind the labels and stock phrases. For the individuals working beyond these trite limits: Thank You. Continue to help your community replace familiar clichés with biblical truth.

---

1. Schaeffer, Francis, *Art and the Bible*, p. 41 "What kind of judgment does not apply, then, to a work of art.? I believe that there are four basic standards: (1) technical excellence, (2) validity, (3) intellectual content, the world view which comes through, and (4) the integration of content and vehicle."

IN THE BEGINNING

God, the divine Architect,[1] laid out the blueprint for the universe, the galaxies, our solar system, and our world. Then as divine Builder, God followed the blueprint to bring the universe into existence. God formed the earth, its land and seas, its flora and fauna, and all its inhabitants, including man and woman.

Have you wondered about the things God created?
Snakes? Why did God need to make snakes?
Mosquitoes? I do not understand their purpose.
The Duckbill Platypus? Was God tiring
when creating this animal?

The Infinite Creator likes to create. Our finiteness limits us from adequately comprehending the Creator's works, but we can grasp the basics. God's works have function and utility, which science studies. Beyond existing for a purpose, God's works include beauty and variety. God enjoys what he brings forth and shares the experience with us, so we, as an audience, may take pleasure in the works with him.

God shared the creativity trait with us, putting inside every person a creative compulsion. In this chapter, we contemplate our creative character. We will also examine many ways creativity is blocked, and how the act of creating develops our ideas.

Let us begin at the beginning with Genesis 1:1.
"In the beginning, God created the heavens and the earth..."

GENESIS

We read Genesis 1:1 as a report of an event, but this viewpoint stays on the surface. We will study this verse by examining the Hebrew words to understand God's creating action.

- The Hebrew word for "beginning" is *rē'řiyt*, meaning: what is first, beginning.
- The Hebrew word for God is *'elohiym*, meaning: God (this word is plural in form but singular in meaning); plural of majesty, with a focus on great power; gods (this is plural in form and meaning); any person characterized by greatness or power, an angel.
- Next, the Hebrew word used for "create" is *bârâ*, meaning: to create as a process resulting in something.
- The Hebrew word for heavens is *šāmayim*, meaning: region above the earth, the place of stars, sky, air, the invisible realm of God.
- The Hebrew word for earth is *'ereṣ*, meaning: world, earth, land, ground, soil, country, region, parts of the earth, territory. When the phrase "heaven (*šāmayim*) and earth (*'ereṣ*)" is used, the meaning is the "totality or whole of creation."

Let us restate Genesis 1:1, "At the start, the beginning, God full of majesty and great in power, brings into being, through creating's process, the whole of creation in heaven and earth."

. . .

The next verses to ponder are Genesis 1:26 and 27, where God on the sixth day said, "Let Us make man in Our image, according to Our likeness...."

- The Hebrew word for image is *selem*, meaning: image (usually referring to an object for worship), an idol.
- The Hebrew word for likeness is *d'mut*, meaning: likeness, figure, image, form, pattern, shape.
- Then Genesis 1:27 reads, God *bârâ* man in his own *selem*... male and female.

We may restate Genesis 1:26-27 to say: God fashioned Man through creating's process—male and female—whose patterning reflected the form and likeness of God's image.

———

Not long after God brought Adam into being, God gave him an assignment: to name all animals and God brought all the animals to Adam so he could do it (Genesis 2:19, 20). Notice the first task recorded about Adam showed him using creativity. This leads me to a question: "How faithful are we with our creativity?" Often, we are poor stewards of the gifts our Creator put in us.

Since God made us in His image, He made us to create. From the time we are born, each person shows God's character through their innate creativity, which flows out of who we are, where thoughts translate to actions. We bring ideas out of our head to exist in reality. Creativity is part of the fabric of God's image in us, which makes us who we are.

THERE IS ALWAYS A "BUT"

"But, but..." This "but" may voice itself in many readers' minds. Do you feel anxiety rising? Is fear taking hold? Being creative scares more people than you would imagine.

This fear says, "But I am not creative! You are talking about someone else!" No, I am talking to you! God put in **your** being the need to be creative. Along with everyone else, you reflect this aspect of God.

WE HAVE AN ENEMY

Did you know we have an enemy called Satan? The Hebrew word, "śāṭān," means adversary, accuser, one who opposes, slanderer, when used as a proper name-Satan is the spirit being who is God's opponent against his creation. And, "satanas," is a Greek word, meaning adversary, opponent, enemy, foe. In the New Testament, "satanas" is interchangeable with the Greek word "diabolos" or devil.

Before Satan became God's opponent, he was one of the top angelic beings, described as bright, full of wisdom and beautiful; he became full of pride and sought to be as God; rebelled against God, along with the angelic hosts he convinced to join him, then the rebellious angels were cast from heaven to earth (Isaiah 14:12-15, Ezekiel 28:11-19, Revelation12:7-9). When I mention our adversary in this book, I do not usually mean the leader of the rebellious angels, but the many devilish spirits using the tactics of their leader to accuse, slander, lie, and oppose God's plans throughout society and people's individual lives.

Our enemy is a thief who comes to steal, kill, and destroy. Jesus came that we may have life and have it abundantly (John 10:10). Keep in mind, the adversary does not like you; in fact, you are hated because you have God's image in you. We can see all the way back at Eden the beginning of the opposition's hatred for humanity; through the Serpent's deception, our genetic make-up was hacked with selfish rationality that we accept as true. Our foe's hate for God is so great that they would destroy God's image on our souls, including its imprint throughout our works and life. Our accusers want to steal God's blessings and life from you and me by killing each area of our life. Our accusers wants us to be ineffective, preferring we stay ignorant through wrong reasonings, all-the-while attacking our confidence, along with blatantly deceiving us. If we follow God, the enemy will try to redirect us back to worldly mindedness; at the very least, away from the truth. Jesus' death and resurrection changed everything. We are not helpless. Jesus gave us his power to destroy the works of the evil one. We are responsible to apply Jesus' resurrection power to the various areas of our life. Creativity is one of these areas.

The Holy Spirit is not passive during the opposition's onslaught of lies, but we often prefer the lies. Ask the Holy Spirit to show you the way Jesus' redemption brings freedom and life to each area of your being, including your creative-character.

When we do not perceive ourselves as God views us, we are not living in reality, but through a fantasy of the accuser's projected images. We will never be authentic believing the enemy's fabrications. Our identity is formed through words and actions of family, friends, teachers, and any other authority over us, including words we speak to ourselves. We often construct our identity based on negative ideas and images, because we believe the lies are who we are. We should understand that we are not our thoughts.

In addition to personal attacks, the god of this world set up society to condition us to its ways. One thing we are taught, creativity is for the gifted. To counter this social programing, I tell all individuals they are creative. Many people answer: "It is not for me, because *I know I am not creative.*" On numerous occasions, when I insist a person is creative, that person argued with me, swearing they are not and never were. The individual who is persuaded they lack creativity embraces one of the accuser's major deceptions. We need not stay in the lies.

CREATIVITY KILLED

We will survey a few ways the opposition keeps us creatively ineffectual. A long time ago, people once thought:

The dance reflected the movement of God, which also moves us upon the earth. The drama presupposes the holy play between God and man. Verbal art is the hymn of praise in which the Eternal and his works are represented. Architecture reveals to us the lines of the well-built city of God's creation. Music is the echo of the eternal Gloria. In the pictorial arts ... the artist makes visible the features of an image which is in the [Creator's] material. [2]

Society no longer perceives the arts this way.

At the personal level, our accusers exploit a biological transition every person experiences. In childhood, between the ages 8 and 10, a child's brain develops and matures. During this stage, the brain transitions from concrete reasoning (this is this) to abstract reasoning (this is that). We may follow a child's development through drawings. The child looks outside their inward imagery (their subjective inner world) to the world around them, and notice things in their environment (objective reality) in fresh ways. They want to draw what they see and depict it as perceived. Many children intuitively can portray what they observe. With others, a teacher shows them the skills to portray their observations. For the rest, they cannot represent what they see. With the child unable to illustrate to their satisfaction, frustration arises and builds through each disappointing depiction. The accumulated frustration eventually crosses a saturation threshold, and then a person gives up art. [3]

Exasperated defeat soaks into the child's soul with each dissatisfied drawing attempt. The enemy magnifies the vexation by adding thoughts to our mind, something like, "You cannot do it; everyone else can, but not you, because you are not creative." Our accuser mixes in shame with the condemnation. Alternatively, a child may begin to learn one of the performance arts, such as music or dance. Frustrated and overwhelmed with the drawing attempts, they devote their creative energy to the other medium of interest.

Children saturated in creative-frustration, who turned away from becoming involved with *any* creative area, embrace what I call, "The Quitting Stage." The Quitting Stage is a verdict people make concluding, "They must not be creative, never were creative, and can never be creative." The result of the judgment is that they shut off a portion of their soul — the creative part. Each individual's decision at this key juncture shapes their life. Following the child's decision to quit, they, as an adult, state, "I cannot draw a straight line" and "I cannot even draw a stick figure." With such thoughts, our opposers reinforce the individual's false conclusion, that they are not creative.

Society declares creative areas are unimportant. Family and friends sometimes repeat the pronouncements. The movie *Sister Act 2* (1993) is an example. In it, the mother of a high school girl who sings very well, tells her that singing does not pay the bills. The mother's fear for her daughter disguised the declarations as protection. Our enemy helps us fashion our cognitive patterns through societal conditioning, which perverts our state of mind and wastes our energy, by diverting focus away from significance. Societal programming instills an automatic desire to compare ourselves to others and their works. Our comparisons stimulate envy, jealousy, and anger.[4] When these emotions are turned inward, they become depression, often intermingled with fear.

The opposite end of the spectrum from rejecting creativity is perfectionism—where everything must be flawless and perfectly done. Perfection arises from fear and is a trap blocking us from freedom. We assume if we cannot do it "perfectly" like an artist, the failure will humiliate us. We determine to not try, by *not* drawing, *not* singing, *not* dancing, etc. We do not take the Holy Spirit's inspiration beyond our thoughts if we cannot execute the inspiration as we imagine we should. This does not mean we withhold from doing the best of our abilities with whatever we are confident we *can* do, as this is good stewardship, but we use our perceived inability as an excuse for not trying or we may not finish what we start. Our perfectionist actions are not based on life nor love but arise from fear, moving us away from the law of the Spirit of life in Christ Jesus, to be under the law of sin and death (Romans 8:2).

Another of the enemy's tactic is for institutional systems to separate individuals from creativity. Our educational system is the most important institution to minimize, disregard, and cripple our creativity. It is easy to observe that children are creative when entering preschool, kindergarten, and first grade. Children's creativity shrinks with each advancement through school (including Christian schools). By high school or college graduation, most people's creativity has reduced to the low-level society considers normal.

School teaches there is one right answer. [5] Did you know most problems, challenges, and puzzles have many right answers? Adults often doubt the truth of this statement. Since the time of the Second Industrial Revolution (late 19th century to early 20th century), factory work and assembly lines have fostered large numbers of workers trained enough for the required work but with limited scope of intellectual and creative thinking. The modern education format taught everyone to perform the same, be good workers, and conform to expectations. Over the last 100+ years, several modifications have come about in education, but without reforming the structure in place for making compliant workers, educated just enough. In school, teachers trained us in the same way they were trained, that conformity and clichés replace creative insights.

Business systems often restrict innovations outside their expectations. Since the last decade of the 20th century, business has pushed for innovation and creativity, but measured efforts have not taken a firm hold. Various innovative methodologies enabled business to grow when a business culture also promotes fresh approaches. However, businesses rarely stimulate creativity beyond the short-term.

Church leaders often educate in the manner taught through schools by propagating conformity and trite expressions. As god of the world's systems, the enemy designs societal systems to influence each area of life away from God's truth. The Church has often shaped itself to imitate secular examples by promoting conformity. Yet we *can* refuse to accept the deceptions. The Bible says, in Romans 12:2: "**not** [to] be conformed to this world, but be transformed by the renewal of your mind, that by testing you may discern what is the will of God, what is good and acceptable and perfect." (emphasis mine)

CREATIVITY EXPLORED

We have talked a lot about creativity. So, what is it? Creativity is a concept difficult to define. Merriam-Webster Dictionary defines creativity as: "1) the ability to create; 2) the quality of being creative." [6] Other dictionaries are not any better.

Brain research has sought to identify and clarify creativity's function, and they found creativity operates in the higher brain functions, observing it includes problem-solving and critical thinking. Researchers recognize new ideas arise as a person freshly considers an existing object or idea. For instance, the well-known account of how Swiss electrical engineer George de Mestral was inspired to invent Velcro from hiking in the woods. Wondering why the cockleburs clung to his pants and to his dog, he looked at the cockleburs under a microscope and realized the hook on the burs held on to the loops of the fabric. [7]

The struggle researchers have with creativity is grasping how we bring forth ideas without an existing reference. This "something from nothing" quality is difficult to measure or quantify. So instead, we will identify a few of creativity's character traits.

Creative people are:

- **Curious**; open, will look at things without labels or judgments.
- **May reframe questions** to consider an idea by asking "why" or "how".
- **Are experimenters**, to problem solve or discover.
- **May be flexible.**
- **Are motivated to create through emotion**, such as love, anger, joy, or sadness.
- **Are sensitive to what enhances or steals creativity**, becoming stubborn against anything that hijacks creativity.
- **May seem rebellious**, labeled as troublemakers because they do not accept the status quo as always correct.
- **Push for development/innovation/change faster than most prefer.**
- **Are undaunted by mistakes**, viewing mistakes as part of the process and not as failure; if a work flops, it may reveal an unexpected, original discovery.
- **Does not link failure to personal condemnation.**

When exercising creativity, people develop many of the traits listed above, because they are engaged in cultivating that part of the Image of God in them which creates. I heard a personal facet of creativity in the 1990s, from pastor and songwriter, Ted Sandquist, as he talked about Romans 13:14 and Ephesians 4:22-24;[8] we, as Christians, can participate with the Living God in our own transformation, or re-creation. In fact, this is something we get to do. We exchange the old nature and its futile reasoning, putting on Christ and His nature.

THE CREATIVE PROCESS

Remember, the Hebrew word *bârâ* means to create as a process resulting in something. This word implies two aspects of creating: the inspiration-thinking side; then the manner of bringing the thought to existence, the doing side. Creating has a Thought phase and an Action phase.

Through the years, psychologists observed the ways artists make works. They noticed commonalities in artists' practices, which they called, *The Creative Process*. The creative process has four basic divisions, labeled as: Impulse, Gestation, Outpouring, and Refining. The psychological examinations fit to the Genesis 1:1 description of creating. The Creative Thought phase encompasses Impulse and Gestation while the Creative Action phase encompasses Outpouring and Refining.

The creative person sifts their experiences of life, their relationships, the ideas bouncing inside their head, through the medium in which they work, processing and distilling it all, to some expressed form. Every work made has resulted from the creative process, even if a maker is untrained in a creative area. Therefore, what does the *Creative Process* entail?

Psychologists observed the creative person has an *impulse* towards an idea. This may come from an assigned problem or from seeing a potential subject or from some stimulus prompted at seeing a drawing, reading a story, hearing a piece of music, or any other source. Frequently, the cause of the idea remains unknown to the person.

After the impulse, the second phase occurs in the form of a period of *gestation*, which may be short, as in seconds or minutes, or long, of years. The maturation could be partially active; or the gestation period may be one in which the impulse seems to lie dormant, evolving and developing in the subconscious mind without conscious awareness, only to rise suddenly to the surface of the mind, structured and formed.

The third and most obvious step of the creative process occurs as an *outpouring*, when ideas come out of the thoughts and take concrete form. The outpouring can appear to be sudden, like a spontaneous outburst; or it can take place as a gradual discovery. Through this creative flood, the person seems to produce without struggle, where emerging forms and relationships come as if the inundation directs their actions.

The fourth and final step is *refining*. The creative person views their work with a critical eye, refines, revises, reshapes, and makes needed changes. Here the creative person views their work almost like an outsider, adjusting it to their own critical standards, which best brings out their conscious intention with the idea.[9]

The creative process is straightforward. We have an idea; we mull it over in our subconscious and/or conscious mind; we get it out of our head in some form; and then we refine the idea's expression. We will move back and forth through *impulse, gestation, outpouring,* and *refining* until the idea reaches its logical conclusion.

At each point in the creative process, we may interact with the Holy Spirit, where we ask questions about the ideas, and seek guidance to bring the ideas out of our head, including the manner of approach. We also may request the Holy Spirit's enabling ability to realize the idea. These prayer interactions during the creative process may energize our works with vitality beyond what we can accomplish.

IDEA PATH

Let us examine the basic trail of an idea by exploring what goes on in our head, leading us to translate the thought into something real. Somewhere in our unconscious, we may have a whim or an urge or a fancy spurring us in a direction, acting as a catalyst to motivate us toward an intent; we then channel the intent to our unconscious imagination. Next, our unconscious imagination ponders over the intent, playing with it, exciting it with energy (hope), pressing forward the energized intent to the conscious side of the imagination as a partial thought. Here we say, "I have an idea." We now consciously imagine possibilities, where the partial thought develops, either in our head or through voicing, drawing, or writing the possibilities. In the conscious imagination, we want to realize the idea's expression. We consider its media-form, and will scrutinize a specific way to achieve the idea through a medium's technical usage (i.e., imagery, compositions, rhythm, words, style, type of movement, etc.). Essentially, our imagination takes inspiration and runs with it, exciting an idea as far as necessary to begin an action, where we realize the idea as a product or service.[10]

It is rare for an idea to pop out fully formed. We must develop the notions to finish an idea's formation, which often happens outside our head. Here, we draw the picture, write the story, make a diagram, try dance moves, notate music, graph the business idea, illustrate the product or invention. Now the proper work on the idea begins. As the idea goes through the creative process, we clarify the image through the medium used to shape it. During this phase of the process, we may ask the Holy Spirit to help us articulate the conceptual notion and furnish the enabling power to accomplish the work.

For an example, let us consider a story's development, to follow an idea through the creative process. From the thoughts in our head, we dash down on paper the story idea. Then we begin expanding it, which could include several paragraphs or pages of scenarios, plot development, locations, characters, and their motives, etc. Next, we build an outline to follow a plot. We ponder the way characters interact with each other, picture characters in various situations, and formulate a general direction of the story while considering how everything will resolve at the end. We may research backgrounds and history for individual characters. At some point, we compose the story. Our story may or may not come out chronologically; we may devise many sections out of sequence and later arrange sections in the outline's order. Or we may begin writing and let the story grow organically. Whatever our method, we develop the story. After the story's outpouring, we must refine it, which is an attempt to make it clear and readable. In refining, we may rearrange sections, edit words that decelerate the reader, add any needed element, remove distracting elements. This may lead to clarifying the impulse-thoughts to better conceptualize plot development or character motivations, translating clearer story interactions. As we jump back and forth through impulse, gestation, outpouring and refining to bring our story to its full development, the audience experiences the intended conceptual and emotional impact.

Every Christian puts the creative process into action when they pray. Beyond reciting rote prayers, each Christian as he or she prays, attempts to hear what the Holy Spirit inspires and directs on a topic. Let's say we pray for a friend and their situation. We may begin praying for the part of our friend's circumstance we are familiar with. Then we open our-self to receive whatever the Holy Spirit impresses upon our mind. Images may arise about our friend and the situation that include details previously unknown to us. If we pray these arising thoughts, they often lead to new or additional images about the situation to pray. We often find our words and thoughts fuller and more developed than anticipated at the outset.

Let us try to understand what we do automatically. We attempt to hear from the Holy Spirit because we have a limited understanding of situations and people. Since God has the best point of view, we open ourselves to pray whatever God gives of his perspective. The Holy Spirit places an inspired image of the situation to pray in our spirit, which then moves to our mind. Then we act, giving voice to the inspired notion as prayer. Prayer is a creative act.

God sends His purpose into our spirit, which was enlivened when we accepted Jesus. Our spirit must have a way to convey

God's inspiration to our mind and heart. The way I picture this process is God's insight received in our spirit transfers to our conscious imagination. We accept or reject the now conscious image. By accepting the inspiration, we transform the thought into action through voicing our prayer.

IMAGINATION

Sometimes we recognize inspiration for what it is, injected images not our own. Or we assume everything in our head is from our self. I believe this is the reason many people are not confident they can hear God; we must distinguish God's images (popularly labeled as "God's voice") from our own. Our imagination is where we sort our thoughts. Imagination is a Middle English/Old French word derived from the Latin verb *imaginari*, meaning *pictures to oneself;* from the Latin base word *imago*, meaning *image.* There are two aspects of imagination which are both considered in this study: imagination as a faculty or ability of our mind to form images and ideas, and imagination as the location in our mind where we manage images.

Our mind's imaging function, labeled as the imagination, is part of a system processing our thoughts; it is where we create, problem solve, dream, and envision what may be. Negatively, the imagination is where we replay hurts, offenses, injustice, and obsess over something or someone. Our imagination administrates image-patterns: visual images (both still and moving), word-patterns, aural-image-patterns of sounds and music, kinetic-image patterns including dance moves and muscle movements, and other sensory patterns involving physical feelings, smelling, and tasting. Our mind sorts the sensory patterns, adding our thoughts and inward images to form new ideas, along with integrating the feeling-associations we subconsciously have about it. The imagination then deposits the loaded image patterns in our unconscious.

When we ponder notions without sensory input, the process

is similar. The images we mull over in our head are charged with associations and feelings taken from our experiences to form a new image-pattern, then deposited in our unconscious-memory. As with dreams, the new pattern-representations, may or may not, contain the same meanings as another memory-image. The emotion-charged-images influence how we perceive ourselves, other people, objects, situations, even God, and form the basis of a belief. Belief-attachments may be true or not true. Afterward, we store the belief-image in the unconscious, until a trigger-response activates the pattern-belief to arise to the subconscious, which influences our emotions and decision processes; the image-pattern-belief may also surface to consciousness.

Often hurts, disappointments, rejections, and fears, including trauma, form a warped image-pattern in us that affects our subconscious decisions and actions. It often takes a revelation to change the distorted pattern. Changing a false belief-image entails replacing the distorted/false representation with God's truth, taking on God's true-image of the issue and of ourselves.

To summarize: our imagination processes image-patterns into ideas. The inspired thoughts in the imagination are charged with energy (hope), so an action can start. Our belief system uses the emotion-charged images to structure our beliefs, whether true or not. We should realize not every notion in our head is our own. As we identify the source of the thoughts, we may differentiate our thoughts from God's thoughts and direction, as well as recognize how they are separate from the enemy's confusions, accusations, and declarations.

INSPIRATION

The English words "inspire" and "inspiration" come from the Latin *inspirare,* meaning, "to breathe into". We may consider inspiration as "breathed into" or "in spirit". Hebrew and Greek languages also present this view.[11]

We receive God's inspired breath through our spirit (as

described above). Then the image transfers to the imagination. Our heart (as the seat of thought and emotion) [12] and mind (as the regulator of the body and processor/developer of ideas) interact with the inspired breath, materializing the image to something accessible. One example to study is Exodus 34 and 35. God filled the heart of the people that made the tabernacle with his breath-inspiration. The people made known the mystery God revealed to them, expressed through the tabernacle and its tangible items.

Inspiration may come from the Holy Spirit, ourselves, or, if we unknowingly opened ourselves to it, demonic injected thoughts. Dr. Jill Taylor is a brain scientist who had a stroke. She eventually recovered and wrote about her experience. [13] She used the term "mind chatter" to characterize the thoughts continually running through our mind. This is where I see our opposition can place thoughts in our head, in the "mind chatter". The Bible does not indicate our enemy has access to our spirit, but signifies that the access point seems to be in the mind. If we do not discern the foe's insertions, we believe the thought-injection is our own idea, and then will build upon it. To be specific, we grab hold of the inserted-thought, to dwell on it.

Whatever the source, we exert creative energy to bring an image or idea out of our minds. Creating is an action, an act. Creativity is a choice, and we choose to create or not create. [14] We have ideas about books, pictures, songs, stories, businesses, or products to invent. Many of us have placed the image on a shelf in our imagination, withholding effort at realizing the ideas. Nothing happens with the Holy Spirit's inspirations if we do not act on them. If we do not follow through with the Holy Spirit's inspiration, we allow the enemy's plans to succeed in our lives.

Keep in mind: ideas are easy. The actual work comes when we choose to achieve an idea. We make choices all the time about the actions we take. Believing the accuser's deceit that we are not creative, we will not do much. We may be busy, but busyness itself can keep us from realizing the Holy Spirit's inspirations. When we do not respond to the Holy Spirit's promptings, he will give ideas to someone else. If God sees a non-Christian artist is faithful with his inspired image better than a Christian artist, he will give the non-Christian artist his inspiration.

Here, at the end of the chapter, let us look back to the beginning. The first way God revealed Himself in the Scriptures is as Creator. The first sentence of the Bible shows God created. At the end of the Bible, in Revelation 21, God brings forth a new heaven and new earth, which is a full "re-creation" of all he made "in the beginning". God brings forth a crowning masterpiece: the "holy city, New Jerusalem," described in verse two as "a bride adorned for her husband". The chapter describes details of lighting and materials and measurement and construction—all the careful considerations of an Artist. It highlights the Creator's attention to detail and the choice materials he selected for the real estate where his throne will reside eternally on the earth.

From beginning to end, God cares about creating and is enthusiastic in his creation. He made us in his image as creators, not only with the ability to create but also with hearts and minds compelled to create. When we exercise our hard-wired creativeness, we become people reflecting our Creator. Creativity is to be displayed in some form throughout every life. Therefore, I believe a Christian is without excuse for living an uncreative life.

Now go, take down the ideas you have put on a shelf in your imagination and ask the Holy Spirit's help to realize them.

---

1. Job 38:4-5 "Where were you when I laid the foundation of the earth? Tell me, if you have understanding. Who determined its measurements—surely you know! Or who stretched the line upon it?"
2. Van Der Leeuw, Gerardus, *Sacred and Profane Beauty*, p. 265
3. Edwards, Betty, *Drawing on the Right Side of the Brain*, I summarized the research Edwards popularized on a child's development, taken from p. 62-79
4. Ecclesiastes 4:4 "Again, I saw that for all toil and every skillful work a man is envied by his neighbor. This also is vanity and grasping after wind." Also, Ezekiel 35:11 "Therefore, as I live, says the lord God, I will do according to your anger and according to the envy that you showed in your hatred against them; and I will make Myself known among them when I judge you."

5. von Oech, Roger, *A Whack on the Side of the Head: How You Can Be More Creative*, p. 24-28, von Oech wrote about "The Second Right Answer" (p. 27), he relayed that our educational system is only concerned with the "right" answer (p. 24). Traditional education training confines our thinking to disregard many solutions to a problem. My art training involved searching for many solutions.

6. *Merrion-Webster.com Dictionary*, *https://www.merrian-webster.com/dictionary/creativity*. Accessed 8 May. 2022

7. *https://www.velcro.com/original-thinking/our-story/*

8. Romans 13:14 "But put on the Lord Jesus Christ, and make no provision for the flesh, to gratify its desires."

    Ephesians 4:22-24 "that you put off concerning your former conduct, the old man which grows corrupt according to the deceitful lusts, and be renewed in the spirit of your mind, and that you put on the new man which was created according to God, in righteousness and true holiness." (NKJV)

9. Mendelowitz, Daniel, *Drawing*, p.423-425 I restate Mendelowitz's psychologically oriented language to everyday language. Other authors have described the creative process with different labels, but I use Mendelowitz's categories as they specify an artistic standpoint, and I think these categories are clearest at describing the creative process itself.

10. The Idea Path description is based on many talks with my father, Dick Sorenson (pastor and counselor-therapist), about mind, memory, and the imagination. Additionally, I use the textbook, *Imagery: Current Theory, Research, and Application* (Sheikh, Anees A., editor, John Wiley and Sons, Inc., 1983) as a reference.

11. Hebrew-"*n'shāmāh;*" breath, blast of breath; by extension, life, life force, spirit; Job 32:8

    Hebrew-"*ruach;*" breath, air, wind, spirit; by extension mind, heart, a person's immaterial self, the seat of life Genesis 1:2, Genesis 6:3, 1 Samuel 16:14, Psalms 34:18, Isaiah 57:15

    Greek-"*pneuma;*" spirit, life, soul, wind, breath; much of the New Testament uses *pneuma*. A few examples are Luke 1:80, John 1:32, Acts 2:17; Acts 6:3; Romans 8:2, 1 Corinthians 12:3, Hebrews 4:12, 1 John 4:1, Revelation 22:17

12. The Hebrew word for "heart" is *lēḇ* and *lēḇāḇ*, both defined as: the inner person, self, the seat of thought and emotion, conscious, courage, mind, understanding. Proverbs 4:20-21 says, "My son, give attention to my words; incline your ear to my sayings. Do not let them not depart from your eyes; keep them within your *heart* [*lēḇāḇ*]". Proverbs 4:23 says, "Keep your *heart* [*lēḇ*] with all diligence, for out of it springs the issues of life".

13. Taylor, Jill Bolte, PhD., *My Stroke of Insight* (2008)

14. Fox, Matthew, *Creativity*, p. 230

❧ 2 ❧

WHAT IS A WORK?

Play is fun, work not so much. Play is more than we imagine. Observe children playing. We may watch a child play at make-believe, which stimulates stories; or combine make-believe with singing to produce a song, or exercise make-believe through a pencil or crayon to draw a picture. In reality, a child's use of make-believe accesses and develops their inherent creativity. Play is more serious than we suppose. Through creativity, aspects of play may appear in our actions, producing a result. When we play, we may work hard at it. Kids like to play. But the required house chores become work. We shape our view of work and play in childhood.

Everyone works for the weekend. Are weekends to recover from our occupations, or do we play so hard we recuperate at our jobs? In our culture, we normally associate work with a job or task which produces an outcome. The reason we work is to pay the rent or mortgage, to buy food and clothing, for cars, bills, etc. Cultural assumptions say work is a necessity and serious, while play is frivolous. Society dismisses the weight of importance that goes into play.

DEFINITION

This chapter will examine the end-product of our creative acts of work or play. Whether we work or play, we channel our energy through an activity. After we make our ideas real, we identify the result as a "work," defined as the outcome of an activity or action. A work is a deed, act, service, product, or thing.[1] Every work brought into reality is because we chose to make it.

YOU AND YOUR WORKS

Since we invest time and energy thinking about the way to realize the ideas in our imagination, including our efforts at making them real, we believe our works are extensions of our being. But this assumption is not true. Specifically, we are *not* what we make or do. Any criticism of our efforts is *not* a critique of us. One skill artists develop is to step back and detach from their work, so they may objectively look at it and make the needed changes at realizing the idea. Therefore, the resulting work is outside its maker. If someone says a work is not right, it is not an attack or a critique of its producer. Your works are not you. You are not your works. Works are by-products of our actions. Whenever we try to connect our identity to our activities and products, it never fits, and deep down, we know it.

A work *may* however denote our traits, either positively or negatively. The Chinese view on this topic states a person's positive and negative nature comes through in the details. A work reflects our non-material aspects, such as inspiration, imagination, ingenuity, courage, energy, strength, and verve. The maker's strength or weakness of character is revealed in the work; in this sense, a work is partially autobiographical, without being linked to its producer's identity. So, because your work is *not* you, any critique of a work does *not* condemn you. Your identity is separate from your works.

I put this issue at the beginning of the chapter, so we recognize the trap quickly without getting caught up in condemnation. We will move forward to find out how the Bible portrays works. As I looked at the way the Bible talks about works, it surprised me how pervasive the subject is throughout the Scriptures.

SAMPLING OF WORKS IN THE BIBLE

For the most part, the Bible is positive in its view of works. Throughout the scriptures, the source of works are God and people. Various Psalms summarize the view to have towards God's works. I will share a couple.

> *I will remember the deeds of the Lord; surely; yes, I will remember Your wonders of old. I will ponder all your work, and meditate on your mighty deeds.*

> Psalm 77:11-12

> *For You, O Lord, have made me glad by your work; at the works of your hands I sing for joy. How great are your works, O Lord! Your thoughts are very deep!*

> Psalms 92:4-5

I encourage you to be like the Psalm writers and contemplate God's works. What are some of God's works? The galaxies and stars in the night sky, the air which we breathe, the winds, clouds, snow, rocks, mountains; water nourishing us and the land, to grow grass, trees, and all other plants sustaining the inhabiting people, animals, birds, and bugs in our world. Then beyond the physical realm are non-material dynamics like love, redemption, mercy, forgiveness, and the way they integrate in people's lives. The Holy Spirit also guides, comforts, and teaches us, which may involve supernatural happenings.

Likewise, people's works involve the tangible and intangible.

We make things and give service as God does; we also develop the intangible in our lives, such as peace, hope, goodness, joy, and faith. This chapter will concentrate on the tangible, material aspects of works.

According to Genesis 6 and 7, God told Noah to build an ark. God gave him the pattern and the basic way to make it, but left many decisions up to Noah. God told Noah to use gopher wood, to use pitch to cover the wood and cracks inside and outside; he gave the dimensions of the ark and instructed to put a roof over it, a door on the side; and then inside to construct three decks, with each deck divided with rooms. Noah was told that two of every animal would come into the ark and that he needed to store food and water for the animals and his family. The account implies that God left the number of rooms up to Noah and gave him responsibility for the room assignments.

Exodus 15 records Moses' response to God's salvation after Israel crossed through the Red Sea. Moses' reaction to God's deliverance is known as the *Song of Moses,* which he and the people sang after their dramatic liberation. Exodus 15 also relays how Moses' sister, Miriam, spontaneously led the women of Israel to rejoice, celebrate, and dance before the Lord with tambourines.

In Exodus 36, God put His spirit on Bezalel and Aholiab, filling them with ability and intelligence, with knowledge and craftsmanship to create all the things God directed them to make for the tabernacle. Bezalel and Aholiab, along with other skilled people, made the Ark of the Covenant, the tabernacle tent curtains, priestly garments, all the furnishings in the tabernacle, the anointing oil, and the altar of sacrifice with the washbasin. God filled every man and woman involved with wisdom, so they were able to fashion every item for the tabernacle.

King David composed songs to the Lord. The Psalms include many of David's songs, covering several categories. The Psalms contain not only David's songs, but other people's. God liked the songs of David and the other psalm-writers enough to include them in the Bible.

The Old Testament has scores of examples covering dramatic acts, music, dance, poetry, architecture, and visual representations. People used their gifts unto God, and God had people use their gifts. Solomon wrote Proverbs, Ecclesiastes, Song of Songs, and built the Temple. God told Ezekiel to bring siege to a representation of Jerusalem, and to lie on his left side for 390 days and his right side 40 days. Nehemiah rebuilt Jerusalem. Joseph and Daniel interpreted dreams and helped run empires. God directed Hosea to marry a prostitute as a prophetic reflection of God's relationship with Israel.

A few works found in the New Testament: Saint Peter opened the door for Gentile inclusion in God's salvation. Saint Paul wrote many letters. Aquila and Priscilla made tents and discipled people. The Apostles and the early church healed the sick, cast out demons, discipled people, taught from the Scriptures, and large numbers died as martyrs. We see Jesus' works in casting out demons, healing the sick, miracles, discipling, and teaching the Kingdom of God has come. Jesus' deep work occurred with his death on the cross, his resurrection out of the grave, and his ascension to the heavens.

JESUS' VIEW OF WORKS

Jesus talked a lot about the subject of works. As we look at Jesus' view, notice how he differentiated between a working-action and the result-of-an-action. In John 4:34, "Jesus said to them, 'My food is to do the will of Him who sent me and to accomplish his *work*'" [Greek *ergon* - anything done or to be done]. In John 5:17 "...Jesus answered them, 'My Father is *working* [Greek *ergazomai* - to work, labor, do, perform, to act, exert one's power, be active, commit] until now, and I am *working* [*ergazomai*]." John 6:28-29, "Then they [the crowd] said to him, 'What must we do, to be doing [*ergazomai*] the *works* [*ergon*] of God?' Jesus answered them, 'This is the *work* [*ergon*] of God, that you believe in him whom he sent'." John 9:2-4, "And his disciples asked him, 'Rabbi, who sinned, this man or his parents, that he was born blind?' Jesus answered, 'It was not that this man sinned, or his parents, but that the *works [ergon]* of God might be displayed in him. We must *work [ergazomai]* the *works [ergon]* of him who sent me while it is day; the night is coming, when no one can *work [ergazomai]*'." And in John 19:30 Jesus said, "It is finished," stating clearly that the work was done. These few verses from the Gospel of John give a good sampling of Jesus' perspective of works. If you are interested in the topic, you may find more verses in John's Gospel and throughout the other Gospels.

OUR FATHER IN HEAVEN

I will interject a thought about Jesus' context. When he talked about God, Jesus characterized the Creator as "Father", as previously stated in John 5:17. In another passage, the disciples asked Jesus how to pray. In Matthew 6:9, he said to pray like this, "Our *Father* in heaven..." (Greek, *patēr,* defined as: one who initiates life, brings into being, produces or generates, procreates, sires, begets.) Father is a personal term, representing a relationship with the one who began life. I see the use of the term "father" instead of "mother" as more connected to creator, through the way "father" initiates the procreation process by sending a seed to a waiting egg housed in the "mother."

We can trace through history the "mother-goddess" concept as early as the pre-Flood neolithic era. The mother-goddess idol is in every culture. Jesus was familiar with the mother-goddess image but tied the Creator to Father, because of a father's specific role in beginning a new life and the unique personal relationship a father has with his offspring. A creator does not always associate with their creations after completion, but a good father does. Jesus emphasized the Creator relates with us as a loving father does.

THE NEGATIVE VIEW OF WORK

Titus 3:5 states that it is "not by *works (ergon)* of righteousness which we have done, but according to his mercy he saved us, through the washing of regeneration and renewing of the Holy Spirit" (NKJV). When *our* works change from being an outcome of what we do to becoming our source, this is idolatry; the Scriptural view of works turns negative when this occurs. Idolatry is the reason for Christianity's love-hate relationship with the visual arts. The Church's attempt to control the impulse of "exchanging the truth for a lie" (Romans 1:25) has condemned visual art as idolatrous, while lumping the rest of the arts similarly. The enemy pushes the point beyond idolatry, where we judge the arts themselves as sinful. This negative perception of the arts maintains the lie the arts may pervert God's image in us.

Let us look at the idolatry issue in Exodus 20, when God gives the Ten Commandments to Moses.

> *You shall have no other gods before Me. You shall not make for yourself a carved image, or any likeness of anything that is in heaven above, or that is in the earth beneath, or that is in the water under the earth; you shall not bow down to them nor serve them...*

Exodus 20:3-5

Since it was first communicated at Mount Sinai, God reiterated in many places throughout the Bible, "not [to] make idols for yourselves or erect an image or pillar, and you shall not set up a figured stone in your land to bow down to it, for I am the Lord your God" (Leviticus 26:1). All the Scriptures addressing idolatry reinforce the view that God is the source, and when we pursue other gods, he removes his protections, allowing us to experience the idol's inadequacy.

An example of this is found in Exodus 32. While Moses was up on the mountain with God for forty days, the people of Israel came to Aaron, saying essentially, "We do not know what is going on with Moses, so make us an idol." Aaron made a golden calf idol in the Egyptian style.[2] The Egyptian cow deity probably represented the goddess Hathor, though some suppose it was Isis. The people of Israel wanted something familiar from the old life in Egypt, even though they had experienced God's miracles.

Is the idol issue still relevant today?
I observed a couple of ways we need to confront the idolatry issue.

First is the contemporary trend to include other religious manners or practices within the Christian faith. In so doing, we do not follow spiritual monogamy. Spiritual polygamy perverts the command to "have no other gods".

The other way Christians attempt to regulate idolatry is by judging the arts through a sacred versus profane view. Dance and drama have a lengthy history in primitive societies, with strong associations to pagan worship, they also convey human and societal perspectives, as well as being used to glorify God. Music has a mixed use of sacred, profane, and secular approaches. Visual arts similarly display sacred, profane, and secular subjects. People seem to correlate visual images with idolic associations more than the other arts, though the other arts also may be tied to idol worship.

Let us look at the word "profane" to help clarify the issue. Profane comes from the Latin—*pro* (before) + *fanum* (temple) = *profanus* (outside the temple, not sacred). Today's synonyms of profane: not sacred, common, secular, vulgar, even blasphemous. Blasphemous is the way we usually define profane subjects. Secular is the modern word for subjects "outside of the temple".

Since we do not want to be polluted by Art's sinfulness, we have withheld God's agape while seeking to regulate the arts' vulgarity. Despite the pious' intent to control sin's corruption, the religious regulations on the arts have not worked; instead, it drives artists further from Christ.

FAITH

Let us finish out this chapter by considering the way faith and works intertwine. We will weigh a few verses from James' letter, in chapter 2, verses 14 to 24.

> *What good is it, my brothers, if someone says he has faith but does not have works? Can that faith save him?*
> James 2:14

> *So also faith by itself, if it does not have works, is dead.*
> James 2:17

> *But someone will say, 'You have faith and I have works.' Show me your faith apart from your works, and I will show you my faith by my works.*
> James 2:18

> *Do you want to be shown, you foolish person, that faith apart from works is useless?*
> James 2:20

Then James gives Moses and Abraham as examples , whose works were the outcome of their faith. Afterwards, in 2:24 James summarizes, "You see a person is justified by works and not by faith alone." James gives Rahab as another example, whose action flowed from her faith.

Biblical faith combines trusting and believing with hope energizing and pressing them together to an action. Without action, we are not exerting faith.[3] We may trust and believe we can, but this in and of itself is not faith.

The question to ask ourselves is, "Where are we directing our faith?" Toward God? Toward objects? Ourselves? Other people? Beliefs or philosophies? Do we direct faith to the unseen or to the known? Our society teaches us to trust and believe in what we materially and sensorially experience. The Bible has an opposite viewpoint, as Colossians 3:1-2 expresses, "If then you have been raised with Christ, seek the things that are above, where Christ is, seated at the right hand of God. Set your mind on things that are above, not on things that are on the earth."

God had people throughout the Scriptures take actions, for as long as it took to complete the act. The eleventh chapter of Hebrews reviews events in the lives of many people in the Scriptures and calls them "heroes of the faith." Hebrews 11:6 gives us the basis in which these "heroes" placed their faith, "And without faith it is impossible to please Him [God], for whoever would draw near to God must believe that He exists, and that He rewards those who seek Him."

Let me share an example of faith in action, to give a fresh perspective. We are driving on a freeway in the middle of winter during a snowstorm and cannot see the road, except for the yellow line peeking through the snow here and there. We come upon a semi-truck (lorry) in the right lane (opposite in Great Britain), then pass the truck in the left lane. As we pass the semi, its tires throw a wall of snow and slush into our lane, over our car's hood, across the windshield, almost more than the wipers can clear, making it difficult to see. We are exercising faith through the action of passing the truck. If we do not pass the truck, we are not exerting faith; we may believe and trust we can, but that alone is not faith. Faith displays itself through the action. We can regard a faith-action as "faithing" (verb form); this is the way the epistles of Hebrews and James approach faith.[4] A faith-action must have a result.

Everyone wields faith, and we usually function in it more than we realize, as the winter driving example shows. All artists use faith to make their works. When making a work, artists trust they will realize the idea in their head, even though it does not exist yet. They hold an image in their mind, not as emotional wishing but factual knowledge, understanding the work will exist once they finish the actions of the creative process—taking anywhere from a few minutes to years. Hebrews 11:1 describes faith-image perception, "Now faith is the assurance of things hoped for, the conviction of things not seen." Do artists use faith more than Christians? This is an interesting idea. You may observe for yourself if it is true. James says in 2:17, "Thus also *faith* by itself, if it does not have *works*, is dead." Faith corresponds to the outcome through which we channel it, which is "the work".

God will judge our works as described in 1 Corinthians 3:12-15. Our works go through a durability test of fire.[5] Reward goes to the works which pass the fire test; if works do not remain, no bonus points.

TO CONCLUDE

James 3:13 says, "Who is wise and understanding among you? By his good conduct let him *show his works* in the meekness of wisdom." The Greek word for "show" is *deiknymi*, which is to point out, to present to the sight, to exhibit, to show, to permit to see, to cause to be seen; to demonstrate, teach, prove, make known, declare.

This verse describes the way an artist displays pictures on a wall, or a composer performs a song they wrote. Displaying or performing works gives evidence the maker completed the creative process.[6] Presenting works declares the maker realized the inspiration. The artist kept an image in mind for however long it took to complete the work. If the artist loses the faith-image during the making process, the work's quality will be poor or left unfinished, unless a new infusion of inspiration fills the artist with a faith-vision, enabling them to complete the work.

Faith is a verb. Faith without action does not exist. Biblical faith has results, which is the proof of things unseen. Therefore, a work is the result, the evidence, of the actions we take.

———————————

1. This is my definition for work. I did not find the dictionaries provided a good enough definition.
2. It is not clear the process used to make the golden calf. It is implied the process was a casting of gold, but equally, the process could have been beaten gold. I will describe both processes. I am more familiar with the casting method but have a theoretical understanding of the beaten process.

    A casting first begins with carving the image in wax. They would have packed clay around the wax-image with some type of support holding the clay together until it dried, maybe cloth or wood. The clay and wax are heated over a fire, so the wax melts out through the vent holes. Then they probably allowed the clay mold to cool down. Once cooled, gold was heated until it became liquified and was poured into the cavity where the wax was. When the gold cooled and solidified, the clay would be removed. Any excess gold from seems and vent holes would be removed. It would have been polished and set on a pedestal or platform made by someone during the casting process. This probably took between 7 to 14 days, even up to 21 days, depending how long it took to carve the idol in wax.If wax was unavailable, they used clay to carve the image and then had to let the clay dry out. They may have fired this clay image, but I do not think so. Once the clay image was dry, they coated the clay image with an oil, or something to allow the mold to separate from the image. Then they packed clay around the image with some type of support to hold the clay together. They allowed the clay mould to dry out, and may have used fire to dry the clay. Once dry, they separated the mold from the image, removed the image, and re-joined the mold together. Here they poured the molten gold into the mold. They would have followed the rest of the procedures described above. The time may have taken 21-30 days, mainly because of all the extra drying time for the clay.

    My understanding of the beaten gold method is that the gold given to Aaron may have been melted down and formed into thin bricks or slabs. During this time the calf would have been carved in wood, as a sculpture. Once the gold bricks cooled, they would have been beaten between sheep skins into sheets—maybe beaten to about 1/8 of an inch thickness. The gold sheets would be pressed around the wood sculpture, beating the sheets to the contours of the image. The gold sheets were pinned to the wood using brass or bronze tacks, which kept the sheets in place. Once the sheets were secure, fine details were applied to bring out the calf's various feature. My guess for the time required is 14-21 days due to the time it would take for beating the gold, even with many people beating.
3. My explanation of faith comes from discussions with my father, Dick Sorenson (pastor/counselor-therapist), regarding the Hebrew and Greek understanding of faith.
4. ibid. My father, Dick Sorenson, used the term, "faithing," to describe the way Greek express faith in verb form.

5. 2 Peter 3:10 "But the day of the Lord will come like a thief, and then the heavens will pass away with a roar, and the heavenly bodies will burn up and dissolve, and the earth and the works that are done on it will be exposed."

6. Psalm 104:31 gives the sense that God enjoys what He created. "May the glory of Lord endure forever; may the Lord rejoice in his works." This a good reminder for us to enjoy our works as well. David wrote many psalms about remembering God's works and about meditating on God's works. If works are not made and shown, then we cannot interact with them. A psalm I like to contemplate every now and then is Psalm 107:23-24, "Those that go down to the sea in ships, who do business on great waters; they see the works of the Lord and his wonders in the deep. God's works are all around us. We do not have to travel very far to see God's wonders."

3

TESTING WORKS

In elementary school, we learn the English language contains homonyms. Homonyms are words with the same pronunciation (and sometimes the same spelling) but different meanings, such as there, their, they're, and to, too, two. The Chinese and Japanese languages also have homonyms, and we understand the correct meaning through a sentence's context. For example, the Japanese Romaji word (Romanized words of Japanese characters) *kami* is god(s)/spirit(s), origami paper, or hair. We understand the meaning from a sentence's placement of tone-accents and its context. The Chinese languages place more accents on words than Japanese's three basic tones, giving more meanings to homonyms. Mandarin, China's dominant language, has 5 tone accents, while other Chinese languages use 9 and 12 tones.

In both the East and the West, we understand meaning through context. When talking with someone, we decipher what they say through our understanding of language and the way they verbally and non-verbally express their thoughts and emotions. We seem to understand each other in conversation. Yet somehow, when experiencing artists' works, we no longer can decipher what we perceive.

Let us try to comprehend the manner we approach meaning

by comparing the way we talk to people, whether speaking with a friend or someone we just met. With friends, we have shared common experiences and often understand their intention through the way they say something. With an unfamiliar person, we do not have a shared history, so explore our commonality through small talk, discovering ways to relate.

But people can be lazy communicators and communicatees. Pursuers of truth search below the surface to uncover the reality and veracity conveyed. My guess at why Jesus shared parables (Matt. 13:10-17) was to uncover who sought the truth. The disciples often asked Jesus about a parable's meaning. Jesus told the disciples many times they should have understood. The disciples eventually asked Jesus to speak plainly to them. When Jesus complied with their request, the disciples still struggled to understand. Are we any different? The disciples at least grasped at Jesus' deep meanings through the stories and word-pictures. Today, we assume Jesus' meanings are at the surface because we doubt anything is deeper.

CURRENT CULTURAL ASSUMPTIONS

Our current postmodern cultural reasoning has shaped us to believe meaning is a fiction.[1]

> ...postmodernism's central goal is to put all assumptions under scrutiny in order to reveal the values that underlie all systems of thought, and thus to question the ideologies within them that are seen as natural. This means that the idea of *authenticity* is always in question in postmodernism. [2]

A postmodern thinker assumes meaning is empty,[3] subsequently, a work is inauthentic. [4] Our cynical view that a work does not communicate a "true" experience blocks us from a genuine encounter with it. We propagate our hollow assumption that works are imitation, a simulacrum,[5] therefore unknowable.

As a result, we think our feelings are the meaning of a work. But we *can* objectively assess works.

Let us consider how to do so. The basic understanding that "the arts express our humanness" is the best argument against the view we cannot comprehend a work's meaning. We are human and can understand the essential needs and desires of other people. We *can* grasp someone else's expressions because works articulate what its maker feels, thinks, believes, wishes, or just wants to convey through a medium. Throughout this chapter, we will touch on a few aspects of evaluating a work, so we may grasp a work for itself.

COMMON APPROACHES

We use one of three approaches to uncover a work's meaning.

1. We try to identify the maker's intention with the work's subject.
2. We only realize our ideas about the work.
3. We may recognize the maker's purposeful idea *and* grasp other meaningful interpretations.[6]

The second approach is how society commonly interprets works. Society indoctrinated us to presume we cannot comprehend a maker's intentions, as their products are assumed empty. Our belief that a work's depth is not deep presumes meaning is superficial,[7] which influences the way Christians interpret the Bible, hear what a preacher is saying, and communicate their views. Our indoctrinated training through society taught us that to understand a work, we must shape its meaning through our biases, involving Class Distinctions, Multi-Cultural labels, Religion, Gender, Ethnicity, Power, Politics, etc.[8] But works are outside our assumptions and biases. To understand a work's meaning, we must use the embedded clues to interpret its intent, and when we do, we align enough to understand what it communicates.

When trying to recognize a maker's intentions, additional thoughts may arise in our mind. The Holy Spirit often operates through this approach. How do we gauge if the extra idea relates to the work? First, view the product/act for its distinct self, in its own perspective. Next, assess the supplemental thought through the work; does the notion relate to the work or not? The created product is the framework where we verify if the thought is random or a supplementary image connected to the work, which may come from ourselves or the Holy Spirit.

The Bible mentions what happens when we do not grasp something through its deliberate viewpoint, or worse, as a pretext (intentionally dismissing the meaning and/or its context in order to enforce our predetermined ideas). In 2 Peter 3:15-18, Saint Peter refers to letters Saint Paul wrote, saying, "...as also in all his epistles, speaking in them of these things, in which are some things are hard to understand, which those who are untaught and unstable twist to their own destruction, as they do also the rest of the Scriptures." Peter encourages them, saying, "You therefore, beloved, since you know these things beforehand, beware least you also fall from your steadfastness, being led away with the error of the wicked; but grow in the grace and knowledge of our Lord and Savior Jesus Christ. To Him be the glory both now and forever. Amen." (NKJV)

Saint Peter warned, two thousand years ago,
not to twist meanings out of context, even with the Scriptures.
If we do, the result is a loss of stability.

PRECONCEPTIONS

We often put more faith in the enemy's lies than God's truth, embracing the "error of the wicked" by viewing everything through our presumptions. Our conjectures blind us, where we cannot perceive works truly, which may also include the Scriptures. The Bible has another example showing how preconceptions filter our experience, even from God. In the Gospel of John, Jesus spoke to a crowd a few days before his arrest, leading to his death on the cross. Let's read what Jesus exclaimed during his talk.

"...Father, glorify Your name." Then a voice came from heaven, saying, "I have both glorified it and will glorify it again." Therefore, the people who stood by and heard it said that it had thundered. Others said, "An angel has spoken to him..."

John 12:28-29, NKJV

The Apostle John identified the crowd as two groups. One group perceived only noise; they doubted God speaks, so assumed what they overheard was thunder. The other understood words but assigned the words to an angel because they also were uncertain God speaks. Each one's bias blocked accurate observation of reality. "Sometimes we want more certainty and think if only God would speak audibly, we would know. But even audible speech is often heard differently by different people."[9]

Preconceptions are obstacles, distorting how we perceive everything around us. Our presumed judgments twist our thoughts and remove us from God's finished work. When we pronounce our judgments, we do not represent Christ and his agape, but the enemy's accusations and condemnations.

Can we recognize when a person assumes a meaning,
placing their predetermined idea on a work?
Yes, we can.

I learned how our distortions block accurate observation when I taught adults a beginning drawing class. For most individuals starting the class, they desired to learn but were skeptical they could, while having some fear about it. I found fear the hardest to overcome because it disorders people's emotions and even alters physical feelings and perceptions.

My usual approach in teaching a beginning drawing class is to put white physical objects on a small table in the center of the room with a light directed at the objects and have people sit at tables six to seven feet away, that surround the set-up, to draw the objects. I, as the instructor, demonstrate how to approach drawing the set-up. Learning to draw by observation, the student discovers how to see truly what they observe, instead of viewing the set-up through their assumptions. This method most often gives the beginner confidence.

I remember three adult students over the years whose fear manipulated their awareness. All three persons started the class seeing normally, without a physical condition affecting their eyes' perception. Each individual had difficulty distinguishing the light-dark relationships on the objects, even when I put my finger on an area we were discussing. This itself is not unusual, as the brain is learning a fresh way of perceiving. As we moved along the normal lines of the learning process, fear filled these students, where they became more emotional, hindering their vision. The most dramatic incident involved a person who had normal vision when they entered the room to start the first class, but during the lesson as fear hit them in waves, overcoming them, their eyesight diminished during the session to blindness at the end; they needed help to leave. Afterwards, they quit the class and their eyesight returned. In these adults, fear controlled physical senses to keep intact the belief "I am not creative."

THE COMPONENTS

When we understand the nature of the arts, it often eliminates one's fears. Let us touch on a few of the components of the arts' fundamental nature. Artists make works that engage Space, containing the sub-dimensions length + width or depth (2-D) + height (3-D), and Time, comprising chronology, movement and/or sequence. All artforms interact with Space and Time in a specific fashion, to convey or communicate its maker's ideas and emotions.

Many books and websites give the relevant data for each art area's elemental ingredients. I will mention several basic elements. **Music** takes place in Time, presented through an instrument's sound and/or person's voice transported through Space, made of *notes* of high or low sounds (*pitch*), swinging in a *rhythm*, arranged along a *melody*, interacting together in *harmony*, at a constant or varied speed (*tempo*), delivering emotions, ideas, and stories. In about half of musical art, words are added. **Drama** takes place in Space and Time through *words and actions* spoken/sung/acted within *characters* to communicate thoughts, emotions, and experiences, following the events of a story line (*plot*) in a certain form (*genre).* **Writing** and reading exist in Time amidst sequenced *words organized* around a story, idea, or *theme*, with *supporting material,* expressed by *word choices, grammar, punctuation, spelling.* The written arts exist in Space through the materials used to hold the words, whether those materials are physical or electronic. **Dance** involves Space and Time interactions with the *body* moving through *space*, while executing a series of *movements* either alone or with others, composed in *rhythmic patterns* along a *beat* with fast and slow *tempo*, delivering emotion, ideas, and/or a story. **Visual Art** arranges Space relationships by using *points, lines, shapes, forms, value, color, pattern*, and *texture,* arranged in a *composition* to portray ideas, people, stories, landscapes, or some other *genre*-specific depictions. Several areas of the Visual Arts, such as sculpture and architecture, interrelate with Time as well as Space. These arts use the elements of clay, wood, metal, glass, concrete, plastics, and any other material. We experience the 3-D works in Time by moving, when appropriate, around and through the piece.

The Visual Arts often confuse us because interacting with Space's sub-dimensions of length and width (2-D) is gestalt communication. To understand how gestalt communication occurs, let us take a picture as an example. An audience looks at the picture and receives the whole of the work's experience, instantly, which contrasts to waiting for a story's, dance's, movie's, or song's sequencing to finish before we may wholly receive the work's experience. The gestalt exchange may take time to process and understand.

Each art form structures its elements into an arrangement that shapes and frames a work into something an audience can approach with understanding. We may identify the work's major elements, such as recognizing cherries are in a cherry pie. Similarly, we recognize a picture uses color and shapes; a dancer's leaps may be fast or slow, light and airy or heavy; an actor or singer accents words uniquely distinct; a story may repeat elements for an intended emphasis.

The way a presenter arranges a work's components influences its perception and guides an audience to flow through the composed assembly. Composition is as important as the ideological-conceptual juxtapositions. The intangible and physical must interconnect before works communicate. One complication interpreting works: the Visual Arts, Dance, and fifty percent of Music broadcast their intentions without words; while the rest of Music, Drama, and Writing relay words to convey meaning. For the works relaying ideas without words, we must exert more energy to discern them than the rest.

STYLE

We express works through stylistic slants. To understand more clearly about style, let us reflect on cultures from various countries as they illustrate stylistic considerations broadly. Culture can be described as a style of living; Italy is different culturally from Kenya or Vietnam or Japan or Morocco or Argentina. Likewise, cities emphasize living life distinctly; in the United States, New York City's culture is stylistically diverse from Boston, or San Francisco, Seattle, Phoenix, Chicago, Atlanta,

Miami, or Charlotte. We may equate style with personality or character.

After we make our work, an audience groups and classifies it into a style category. Several divisions are: Romantic, Classical, Modern, Post Modern, Regional, International, Jazz, Rock, Country, Christian, etc. Style is an artificial classification, meaning more in people's minds than the works themselves. The groupings are inaccurate projections on a work, but they provide a means for an audience to connect through generalization.

To simplify, style is the way we do things.

SYMBOLISM AND METAPHORS

In order to convey the deeper aspects of our ideas, we may use more advanced factors to invoke images which expound on and clarify the tangible and intangible concepts presented. The technical term is "figurative language". The figurative images we use most are Symbols and Metaphors, which convey a wider range of meaning for the ideas we present. Culture has labeled most figurative language as metaphorical. We do not have to be *sharp as a tack* to understand metaphorical expressions.

We will explore symbols first. On the doors of a restaurant's toilets are plaques with a male and female figure. The symbols are not photographs of the people using the toilets, but a generalized representation for the male and female populace who may use the facility. As political correctness extends itself, society adds symbols to restroom plaques for people not identifying with their biological maleness or femaleness.

Our society surrounds us with symbols, and there are so many that we no longer notice them. Pictures, numbers, movements, sounds, and even the words you are reading are symbols used to stand in for ideas and emotions, but are not the actual thing. The definition of symbol is: a sign, a representation for something, which may denote ideas, emotions, objects, services, companies, people groups, countries, etc. A business logo signifies a company, and a national flag, a country. Any memorial is a symbol, reminding us of an event, a person, or a group. Holidays are memorials established for symbolic remembrance.

Next, we will touch on metaphors. Metaphors link symbolic images to convey a larger idea, giving a fresh way to perceive the idea; specifically, a metaphor connects two unique items but says the connecting-something *represents* something else. Let us differentiate metaphor from simile: a simile directly compares two separate things and begins with "as" or "like" to describe a *resemblance*. Analogy also associates two entities, based on their being alike—for instance, showing the *comparison* of an atom and the solar system. Here are a few common metaphors: my sister is the black sheep of the family; since college, I have been a night owl; did a bomb go off in the room?; she has a heart of gold; they don't have a snowball's chance in hell; and he could not see the forest through the trees.

The Bible abundantly uses symbolism, metaphors, similes, analogies, and other types of figurative language. I will limit our examination to a few similes and metaphors.

An example of simile usage in the Bible is Isaiah 1:18, "'Come now, let us reason together,' says the Lord; 'though your *sins are like scarlet*, they shall be as *white as snow*; though they are *red like crimson*, they shall become *like wool*'." And in Matthew 13, Jesus used similes in talking about the kingdom of God/heaven, saying it is *like* a mustard seed (v. 31), *like* leaven in dough (v. 33), *like* a hidden treasure (v. 44), *like* a fishing net that gathers fish of every kind (v. 47).

Some biblical metaphors from the Old and New Testaments:

- Psalms 18:2—*The Lord is my rock and my fortress and my deliverer, my God, my rock, in whom I take refuge, my shield, and the horn of my salvation, my stronghold.*
- Psalms 23:1—*The Lord is my shepherd....*

- Isaiah 9:2—*The people who walked in darkness have seen a great light; those who dwelt in the land of deep darkness, on them has light shone.*
- Mark 1:16-17—*Passing alongside the Sea of Galilee, he [Jesus] saw Simon and Andrew the brother of Simon casting a net into the sea, for they were fishermen. And Jesus said to them, "Follow me, and I will make you become fishers of men."*
- 1 Corinthians 12:12—*For just as the body is one and has many members, and all the members of the body, though many, are one body, so it is with Christ.*

Judaism and Christianity use symbolism and metaphor. For instance, in Exodus, God instituted Passover. Every year, Jewish families eat a Passover Seder dinner, to remember God's deliverance from Egypt and remember how God brought them through the year. Each part of the Passover dinner is a symbol of the Exodus story, helping participants connect with God's goodness in the past and for the present. Jesus established Communion during his last Passover Seder before he went to the cross; he used elements in the Passover dinner as metaphors to remember and identify with his death and resurrection.

Now as they were eating, Jesus took bread, and after blessing it broke it and gave it to the disciples, and said, "Take, eat; this is my body." And he took a cup, and when he had given thanks he gave it to them, saying, "Drink of it, all of you, for this is my blood of the covenant, which is poured out for many for the forgiveness of sins."

Matthew 26:26-28

Today, Christians continually apply Jesus' symbols[10] to their lives as we remember and identify with Christ through the Communion/Eucharist experience. Jesus' audience, when they listened to his parables, seemed oblivious to the larger meaning conveyed. If we do not grasp how works incorporate figurative language of symbols and the metaphoric, then we will likewise be clueless. A Christian who reads the Psalms, Proverbs, Song of Songs, the writings of the Old Testament prophets, Jesus' parables, the Apostles' letters, and the Revelation of John should have no problem understanding Art since the Bible uses metaphors and other such figurative language. But most Christians stay at the surface with the arts and do not penetrate its metaphors. So, I wonder if Christians *do,* in fact, comprehend their biblical readings with its layered meanings.

As we seek to understand biblical figurative language, observe the way a verse's context contains its metaphorical meaning. Our everyday use of figurative language also ties meaning to its context. Symbolism and metaphor surround us, supplying us with the resources to understand the creative message expressed in works of art.

MORALITY

As mentioned in the first chapter, the people who believe the enemy's lie "they are not creative" bury the creative portion of their soul. Once we embrace the "Creative Quitting Stage" we judge works through a favorably perceived morality. Christians commonly approach works as moral or immoral, and in doing so, misunderstand the works of art they happen upon.

An excellent example is the movie *Footloose* (1984). *Footloose* portrayed life in a small town. The town's pious rules stifled the newly arrived high school boy from the big city. The local pastor led the pious community. A few years before the teen's arrival, the town classified dancing as immoral and outlawed it within the city limits. In a thought-provoking speech, the new kid challenged the false moral perspective of the town, so the town council would change the ordinance banning dancing within the town limits, which would allow the high school to hold a senior prom. The town council did not change the ordinance. The students held their prom outside the town's limit. The new kid asked the pastor's permission to take his daughter to the prom and received it. The movie ended in dancing, celebrating youth and life, and implied freedom coming to the town. *Footloose* effectively illustrated how Christians reproached social dancing in the 1980s; and the movie accurately reflected the surrounding censorship issues of its time. Years ago, Christian culture considered dancing immoral, but today, we acknowledge numerous ways a Christian may dance.

And, Christians have also condemned secular music as immoral, especially if the beat was too fast. The music style denounced then is now a style of music within the Christian music genre. Condemnation often centers on rejection of style.

Let me say, there are right and wrong actions which may be moral and immoral. A style of art itself is neutral. Assuming style equates to goodness or wickedness, we may deem anyone with a Southern accent as full of iniquity, or conversely, all "Yankees" as evil. Our accusations and condemnations are false presumptions taken from the enemy, who seeks to prevent us from receiving from God through the "various and sundry" means in which He is revealed and enjoyed (Hebrews 1:1-3, KJV).

Some works may depict subjects that align with our point of view. Other works may challenge our assumptions. Still other works may make a blasphemous display of subjects; for example, Andres Serrano's well-known photograph, *Piss Christ* (1987). How should we respond to the works we encounter? To begin to answer this question, we need to contemplate the underlying issues.

A single work may uncover some of its creator's character; but an individual work is only a momentary snapshot. Francis Schaeffer pointed out in *Art and the Bible*, the artist's body of work shows its maker's worldview.[11] We may or may not grasp a maker's perspective. As we try to understand the experiences a work offers, we must recognize that our preconceptions can blind us from truly perceiving a work as its maker intends. If we cannot objectively discern a work's aesthetic conceptualization (explained further in this chapter), then we can only inspect a work through our perceived moral "rightness" or a favored agenda. So, again, how should we respond when we encounter a blasphemous work? Let us explore further background.

JUDGING AND TESTING

The Bible supplies us with the correct approach for assessing a work of art. Jeremiah 17:10 says, "I, the Lord, search the heart, I test the mind, to give every man according to his ways, according to the fruit of his deeds." We are not the one that give to others according to "the fruit of their deeds." But we can examine people's resulting deeds, i.e., works. We will weigh two distinctive attitudes/approaches, described through Hebrew and Greek words the Bible uses for judging and testing, then apply these methods to the arts.

Let us define judging and testing. Judging involves deciding upon something with a concluding pronouncement of right or wrong. Judging wraps itself around a perceived morality. Testing is a way to assess and evaluate quality, genuineness, reliability, performance, even character. Morality is *not* attached to testing.

Since most of us do not know off-hand the Bible's languages, let us narrow our review to the Greek words for judging and scan a few verses in the New Testament using the words. If you are interested in an in-depth study, I placed the Hebrew words for judging in the endnotes, along with a sampling of verses from the Psalms.[12]

The Greek words for judge in the Bible:

- *krinō*—to separate; to make a distinction between; to exercise judgment upon; to judge; to assume censorial power over; to pass judgment; bring to trial

- *anakrinō*—to shift; to examine closely; to scrutinize, scan; investigate
- *diakrinō*—to separate, sever; to make distinction or difference; confer a superiority; to examine; to discriminate; to dispute, contend; be in doubt
- *krima*—judgment; a sentence or award; condemnation; punishment
- *kritēs*—a judge, magistrate; ruler

A few verses that use the Greek words:[13]

- Matthew 7:1-2—*Judge (krinō) not that you be not judged (krinō). For with the judgment (krima) you pronounce you will be judged (krinō), and with the measure you use it will be measured to you.*
- 1 Corinthians 4:3—*But with me it is a very small thing that I should be judged (anakrinō) by you or by any human court. In fact, I do not even judge (anakrinō) myself.*
- James 2:4—*Have you not then made distinctions (diakrinō) among yourselves and become judges (kritēs) with evil thoughts?*

Now, let us briefly investigate how the Bible refers to testing, then how it differs from judging. The Hebrew words used for testing are in the endnotes, including a sampling of verses.[14]

The Greek words for testing:

- *dokimazō*—to test, assay metals; to prove, try, examine, scrutinize; to put to proof, tempt; to approve after trial, judge worthy; to decide upon after examination, distinguish, discern
- *dokimion*—by means of which anything is tried, proof, criterion, test; trial, the act of trying or putting

to proof; approved character

- *dokimos*—proved, tried; approved after examination and trial; acceptable
- *adokimos*—unable to stand a test, rejected, refuse, worthless
- *eimi*—to be; to exist; be
- *peirazō*—to make proof or trial of, put to the proof, whether with good or mischievous intent; to attempt; to try, subject to trial; tempt; test
- *peirasmos*—a putting to the proof, trial; direct temptation to sin; trial, calamity; affliction
- *pyrōsis*—a burning, conflagration; a fiery test of trying circumstances

Some verses using these Greek words:[15]

- 2 Corinthians 13:5-6—*Examine (peirazō) yourselves, to see whether you are in the faith. Test (dokimazō) yourselves. Or do you not realize this about yourselves, that Jesus Christ is in you?—unless indeed you fail to meet the test (adokimos)! I hope you will find out that we have not failed the test (eimi)!*
- 1 Thessalonians 5:21—*Test (dokimazō) everything; hold fast what is good.*
- Hebrews 3:8-9—*Do not harden your hearts as in the rebellion, on the day of testing (peirasmos) in the wilderness, where your fathers put me to the test (peirazō) and saw my works for forty years.*
- James 1:12—*Blessed is the man who remains steadfast under trial (peirasmos), for when he stood the test (dokimos) he will receive the crown of life, which God has promised to those who love him.*
- 1 Peter 4:12—*Beloved, do not be surprised at the fiery trial (pyrōsis) when it comes upon you to test (peirasmos) you, as though something strange was happening to you.*

We explored judging and testing because they affect how we discern people and their works. As we survey the definitions and verses with judging, we see it separates according to real, imagined, or perceived moral rules, even Scriptural rules (taken from a knowledge of the tree of good and evil), and we assume we have censorial power to pronounce judgment upon others. There is no love with judging. People's judgment usually amounts to condemnation, with accusation and shame thrown in, if we feel generous.

1 Thessalonians 5:21 gives us the approach of how we regard what people say and do: we *dokimazō* (test, examine, scrutinize, discern, put to proof), then hold fast to what is worthy while letting go of the rest. Testing weighs, examines, and assays a work's quality or genuineness, while assuming whatever weakness exposed will be addressed. Testing does not morally consider each person's actions. The aim of testing is for an individual, and by extension their works, to pass the test.

We naturally judge from our understanding of good and evil and assign a motive to people for their actions. The Bible does not positively endorse our judging. In fact, Saint Paul says to not judge (*krinō*) in Romans 2:1-4, and in 1 Corinthians 4:3, he said he does not even judge (*anakrinō*) himself. Saint James , in James 4:12, goes a step farther, saying there is only one Lawgiver and Judge, and who are you to judge (*krinō*) your neighbor?

EVALUATING WORKS

The question becomes: can we evaluate without judging?
Yes, we can.

Let me share how we test a work:

- First, we determine a work's "Content," the idea or subject matter, i.e., what it is about. We are *not* judging if the subject matter is morally correct; if we do, we place a label on the work that restricts us from seeing it for itself. To recognize content, we *only* discover the idea; we are *not* judging it.

- Next, we notice a work's "Expression," *the way* a maker conveys the idea. To help shed light on a work, we ask ourselves: Did the maker's *expression* realize the thought? Here we study *how* the maker articulates the Content—through its arrangement of elements, style, emphasis, or accents, including anything left out. We contemplate *how* Content is communicated, and weigh if the maker brought out its fullness; or did the maker present the idea through a clichéd form? When we recognize *how* a work Expresses its Content, we go beyond a surface awareness, drawing nearer to its true meaning.

REMAKES

To better understand how Content intertwines with Expression, let us look at remakes. We interact with recreated materials every day: remakes of songs (covers), stories (adaptations), movies (remakes and adaptations), pictures (copies, reproductions, remakes), etc. A remade version may keep the original's content while uniquely presenting it, or might change the content *and* uniquely present it. And there are many works that replicate the original without including its spark of life. The difference of approach condenses to a philosophical assumption of either being faithful to the work or a belief the presenter is a co-creator who may alter a work according to their own notions. Distilling the success or failure at presenting remakes amounts to preserving a work's vitality—its inner fire. The remade work succeeds if it includes the vital dynamic ignited in the original. When we alter, diminish, or disregard an original's essence, an audience dismisses the remade work.

Consider how a singer sings a song, for instance, *Amazing*

Grace. We have heard many versions of the hymn, some strong and some weak, rendered through many styles. Imagine singers portraying *Amazing Grace* through styles of Country, Jazz, Rock, Reggae, or Rap; the singers sing the same words, but each style influences the manner a singer presents the song. A style has minimal influence on shaping content. When we convey content, we must concentrate on *how* a work communicates its ideas. Listening to a singer sing *Amazing Grace*, if they do not pass on the song's intent and its passion, the presentation is unsuccessful. Therefore, to relay the work's spark, the singer must communicate the song's wholeness, not just sing the words.

CONTENT/EXPRESSION COMMON SCENARIO

Whether we experience original works or covers/adaptations of works, we use the same evaluation method: we examine *how* a creator Expresses a Content.

Let me share a common scenario to show we already use this evaluation. Have you ever walked out of a cinema after watching a movie and thought or said to someone, "It was a good idea, but they did not pull it off?" In this scenario, first we identified the movie's basic idea. We have a natural inclination to identify a work's subject; in essence, we want to know what something is about. Many works may take time to uncover their ideas, which is the manner Jesus used in giving parables. After pinpointing a movie's subject, we may recognize its potential but observe that the moviemakers missed realizing its promise. Many movies fail to meet their promise, and many more ignore significance, because they target the lowest common denominator in their audience. When we spot a movie's disconnect, it is here we identify, "They did not pull it off."

We will detect a work's negative aspects, *and* we can notice its positive areas. We credit how a Content and its Expression symphonically combine, through acknowledgment. In several comedy clubs, I heard comedians tell relationship jokes. I remember three separate incidents where a person behind me responded to a joke by yelling, "Yeah!!!" To break apart the interaction, the way the comedian told the joke expressed the idea in such a way its truth resonated with the person behind me, and they reacted, appreciating the joke's reality. They intensified their acknowledgement of the joke through the emphasis of their response.

We appraise everything made in the arts—stories, pictures, music, dance—by considering *how* a Content and its Expression come together. In fact, we may use this test to scrutinize any product or service people create. We examine every work in every form according to the way a maker Expresses a Content.

GENESIS

The first chapter of Genesis implies this evaluation of looking at an idea through the way it is realized. At the end of each day's creation, we see the phrase, "And *God saw* it was *good*."

The Hebrew words used are, *elohim rā'āh ṭāḇaḇ*.

- *ṭāḇaḇ* is a verb, to speak.
- *rā'āh* is the general word for visual perception and is:
  to see, look, view, to realize, know, consider; to
  become visible, to appear, to show oneself; to be seen;
  to cause to see, show; to be shown.
- *Elohim* is the word for God.

Let us translate this phrase as: God knowing, realizing, spoke his view seen; beholding, approving, enjoying his visible word.

God aesthetically contemplated what He created; seeing it all as itself—as *rā'āh* describes. When we explore the way a maker expresses an idea, the work becomes visible to us, as itself, and we view its strengths and weaknesses. We "see" a work for itself.

At the end of each day of creation, God *rā'āh* what He made. Here, God was not in the creating mode but took on the role of an audience, where he observed the created works, appreciating how everything symphonically and harmoniously connects. God took a moment to examine his creation and exclaimed the knowing view seen: It is good.

I want to emphasize that God saying, "It is good" was not giving a moral judgment, but God viewed creation through *rā'āh*. When everything works, we often say it is "good," not in a moral sense but an aesthetic or practical sense. Conversely, if something does *not* work or is deficient, we label it aesthetically as "bad," or we perceive it somewhere in-between good and bad. We can detect when a work comes together and when it does not.

Let us distinguish aesthetic from moral perception.

> The relationship between aesthetic and moral judgments is close, but the distinction between them is important. One factor of this distinction is that while aesthetic judgments are mainly positive, that is, perceptions of good, moral judgments are mainly and fundamentally negative, or perceptions of evil. Another factor of the distinction is that whereas, in the perception of beauty, our judgment is necessarily intrinsic and based on the character of the immediate experience, and never consciously on the idea of an eventual utility in the object, judgments about moral worth, on the contrary, are always based, [even] when they are positive, upon the consciousness of benefits probably involved.[16]

Aesthetic evaluation involves more than "perceptions of good or bad". When people pronounce judgments on a work's morality, this stems from mulling over a message through its perceived right-ness or wrong-ness, along with checking how it promotes their group's ideology. There is no agape in such moral judgments.

YOU MAY DISAGREE WITH WORKS

We *can* see a work for itself. We may not like or agree with whatever a work conveys, and this is okay. Likewise, we may disagree with a friend. And we may differ with the preacher. Understanding a work is not the same as approving its idea.

Let me add one more thing about grasping works. When we try to comprehend what an individual work conveys, if we find we disagree with a perceived message, it is *not* personally attacking us. Remember in Chapter Two how we identified the enemy's trap of connecting our identity to our works. On the flip side of this, we, as an audience, are not tying our identity to the works of other people. Agreement or disagreement with a work does not give it control over us. We have power over ourselves in how we respond. We are *not* tossed around in the sea of life, unstable and driven to wherever the wind blows us because of a lack of faith (James 1:6-8). Our faith is *not* in people, their actions, or treatment of us, nor do we base faith on the words or works of others. Rather, our faith is on Jesus. Our identity and power come through Jesus as an overcomer (Revelation 1-3; and 12:11); we overcome all that society imposes on us and that we place on ourselves, because God adopted us into his family, and we are children of the King. Therefore, what people put forth does not dominate us, and disagreeing with a work's message is not a big deal.

LOOKING BEYOND THE SURFACE

We understand that the purpose of the arts is to communicate ideas. Let us parallel this with normal human speech because the intention of talking is to transmit our thoughts. We talk about everything, from bad jokes to shopping lists, from politics to work, memories, and the beauty we observe around us, car repairs, housework, plans for the future, food, school, the opposite sex; and sometimes we inform others of God's interactions in our lives. Do we expect the arts to compensate for our mundane babble? Maybe subconsciously we do. The subjects conveyed through the arts also may be ordinary: jokes, politics, memories, beauty, family, romance; and sometimes the spiritual. The arts communicate the topics we commonly share, and a maker will present the same true and false notions towards each subject matter as held by their audience.

When makers of art *only* express themselves, they rarely communicate, instead they spout-out. Self-expression broadcasts its utterance but, at best, limits itself to be a "one-liner". What is our self-expressed drivel? This is a good question to ask ourselves. Self-expression is often white noise, easily forgotten once experienced.

Art may use self-expression, but Art requires more than giving voice to thoughts or feelings. We direct our intention in a specific manner that expresses a Content to which others may respond or connect. Let me emphasize this point, the work we make is to express its larger, meaningful idea in such a way that an audience's experience is engaging.

Through societal indoctrination, we assume everything is on the surface. God does not work this way. The way God operates is deep and wide, which is hard to fathom. "God is the faithful God who keeps covenant and steadfast love with those who love Him and keep His commandments, *to a thousand generations*" (Deuteronomy 7:9, emphasis mine). We have a hard time remembering what God did in our life yesterday, let alone a year ago or twenty. Our faulty memory is the reason the Scriptures say over and over and over, to remember God's faithfulness, to remember his works. But we usually stay at the surface.

If we want to be trustworthy communicators, we go beyond pushing messages at people and must stop spouting cliches. For Christians, this means we incorporate into life the revelations of Jesus' love and goodness to us. When we apply the Holy Spirit's revelations, we show ourselves the practicality of God's truth. Afterwards, we share as a witness. Artistic mediums provide a way to express the revelations.

ON TO LIFE

How do we convey God's inspirations through artistic mediums? This is a central question for every creative person. Writing a story of the revelation of God's love is straightforward. An interpretive dance may easily convey God's love to its audience. Both examples stay on the surface because their communication is apparent. What if our subject does not directly relay the obvious but is indirect, even subtle; should we quit working in this manner? No. Jesus operated in this way.

We must convey more than the normal superficiality by swimming in the deep, beyond the shallows. The way I see through this mystery is for Christians to go beyond a message, relaying through our works vitality and Holy Spirit infused life. This is not easy. Hebrews 6:1 says, "Therefore let us leave the elementary doctrine of Christ and go on to maturity, not laying again a foundation of repentance from *dead works* and of faith toward God" (emphasis mine). For works to go from dead to something vital, they must be filled with life. Vital works fully express its content, craft-wise (where each element has a dynamic interlocking tension throughout its composition), and idea-wise (in the way we express an idea). Both areas must actively function together in an orchestral harmonious interconnectedness, which is the prerequisite before vitality/life attaches to a work. This is creative maturity.

Let me give some background to show how we address the dead works issue. Life is full of energy. The Greek, Hebrew, and Latin languages associate life with breath and spirit: *pneuma* (Greek)-spirit, life, soul, wind, breath; *ruach* (Hebrew)-breath, air, wind, spirit; *spiritus* (Latin)-breath, breathing, life, spirit. All three languages distinguish activity-movement as different from spirit-life. Let us narrow down to one language, Latin, which is the foundation for a lot of our English words.

We will examine the words *spiritus* and *anima* and how they differ conceptually:

- *Spiritus*-breath, breathing, life, spirit; it is what energizes our being.
- *Anima*-life, soul; it is the movement-activity of the soul.[17] *Anima* is the root of the English words "animate" and "animal." Let us look at how *anima* shapes the word "animate," by combining several dictionary definitions of "animate": having life; possessing or characterized by activity, movement.

The power that runs and operates our being to life is *spiritus*. *Anima* describes the activity or character that *spiritus* empowers, i.e., being animated. We already understand when something is animated as opposed to alive. Robotics provides an example of what it looks like for something to be active (anima) but without life (spiritus). Science fiction speculated on what might happen if spirit could empower robots or the inanimate. Scientific research in artificial intelligence (AI) has attempted to blur the lines between animate-ness and alive-ness, but I doubt they will impart alive-ness, no matter how realistic robotic AI becomes.

Through the ages, from Europe to Asia, global cultures recognized the universal concept that works may be energized with vitality and life (spiritus). As early as the 5th century, China codified artistic criteria. The First Principle is *ch'i-yun sheng-tung* (Wade-Giles);[18] which translates in English as "resonance or vibration of the vitalizing spirit and movement of life." This was the goal every artist strove for, to have their works "resonate with the eternal vitalizing spirit, moving with life". European countries have diverse words for describing a work's vitality, such as "sublime," but commonly recognize when a work is substantial enough to be a masterpiece, where it becomes more than its materials and arrangement, to possess vital energy.

PNEUMA'S PRECONDITIONS

As makers, let us ask ourselves, "How do we fuse *pneuma/ruach/spiritus* into our works?" If *pneuma/ruach/spiritus* is to fill works, we must satisfy some conditions.

Proverbs 11:1 states, "A false balance is an abomination to the Lord, but just weights are His delight." (NASB) We can consider this verse as the first condition. A balance may relate to more than a scale. I see it as applicable to anything we do, and it may be a guide to how we make and present our works. The verse shows God dislikes false dealings. Beyond this surface perspective, we may use the verse to ponder how to distribute a work's weight-placement. The weight of a work's Content and its Expression should be in equilibrium. If the weight is one-sided, placed mostly on Content, message is the primary element and is propaganda. Propaganda discounts the weight of an idea's Expression. Propaganda is lifeless (including Christian propaganda). If most of a work's weight is on Expression, there is not enough substance to keep us interested. When Expression carries the majority of the weight, we call the works "decoration," which has little to no substance and stays in the background. Or the works are "one-liners," which have some substance but not enough to hold our attention beyond the initial understanding, staying as decoration.

When a work's weight is one-sided or out-of-balance, synergy cannot generate between its parts. Intuitively we know it and describe the work as "bad". For us to impart *pneuma* to our works, the idea/message must be in equilibrium with its expression, both parts in a symphonic harmonious interplay. When a work's Content is in symphonic balance with its Expression, we recognize it as a "good" work. Through the years, I observed God imparts his life into our work only when a work is balanced—its elements are in harmony, in unity.

The other condition needed before *pneuma* may occur is more intangible. We must actively, on purpose, make a work in such a way vitality fills it. This is not so easy. Not everything we make will breathe. But we *can* regularly imbue works with life. Affixing the intangible to our material is perplexing, and there is no formula to follow. However, we can grasp some of this mysterious connection.

There are three ways vitality may permeate works:

1. When the artist imparts their soul energy.
2. When they intentionally meet with the Holy Spirit throughout the creative process, where their work takes on the inspired breath blown through them.
3. God places his life and spirit in a work for His purposes.

Non-Christians will often fill a work with their soul energy, and we respond to their works, as with the paintings by Pablo Picasso (1881-1973), Salvador Dali (1904-1989), Andrew Wyeth (1917-2009), and Chuck Close (1940-2021). We respond to a picture's energy, either positively or negatively. Standing before paintings in a museum, we may notice many works display a dynamism. Not everything in a museum has life. God's Spirit may have attached to a few works in museums, but typically, the force we observe is soul-energy.

When God's Spirit attaches to works, we encounter them differently than through soul-energy, such as *Pilgrim's Progress* (1678) and Handel's *Messiah* (1741). When we watch movies in a cinema, hear songs on the radio or our playlist, or read novels, can we distinguish where a work's energy is from? A work draws an audience according to the amount of vitality it contains. If a work does not have vitality, then it is dead, a husk, a hollow form. The route used to fill a work with life is less important than the fact life energy infuses the work. Presenting vitality is a critical issue for Christians. We will naturally convey our soul-energy through our works unless works are trivial or shallow. People respond to works filled with soulish energy; but a greater impact occurs when works include God's power. Let us keep in mind that when non-Christians present energized works to the public, then Christians should also. But we presented only messages. God imparted to us a new life through the cross and Jesus' resurrection; our concern is for life. Therefore, our works are to transmit both vital energy and dynamism, *pneuma* and *anima*. Let us not present dead works. So, we should ask ourselves: Do we make works in a way that God *will* place his vitality in them?

ART

Now we can answer the question from the Introduction: When does a work become "Art" with a capital "A"? A work expressing an idea is art. It is easy to recognize good works as art. But even a work with content misaligned to its expression and labeled as "bad art," is still art. Craft can confuse us because craft can either become art or stay as craft. Craft is utilitarian in its purpose; its products meet functional needs. Quilters make quilts. Potters make containers and cups. Woodworkers make chairs, tables, and cabinets. Techniques are important in craft, as well as in the arts. Craft celebrates materials, appealing to a craft's aesthetic. Where craft crosses over to art is when a maker moves the work's purpose from utility to the expression of idea.

LASTLY

Let us move on to maturity. We can regard people's works in their own right, including the shortcomings and virtues present. Test every work by examining its *Content* to discover its idea, then observe the way the work *Expresses* the Content; did the maker "pull it off"?

We can understand a work's meaningful perspective. If we ignore a work's context, we may withdraw to deciphering the work through our biased moral judgments, or an associated fantasy. Many works take time to comprehend because they are not immediately obvious. Does our taste stay superficial? We surround ourselves with trivial products, easily ingested and with little flavor; "baby food." Our substantial creations may contain conceptual layers of meaning, as do many of the Psalms. We are to grow up to maturity, eating meat, chewing, releasing flavors to the taste buds before we swallow to digest. With good artwork, we chew on it, savoring the flavors.

Therefore, creating works is not about plopping something out. When we create, we arrange a work's elements to interact in a vibrant balancing tension, working with an awareness of its expression. And hopefully, we imbue the work with vitality. As we put into practice the skill for testing all things, remember to hold fast the good and let go of the rest.

---

1. Stuken, Marita, Cartwright, Lisa, *Practices of Looking*, Quote reproduced with permission of the Licensor through PLSclear. p. 252. "One of the primary aspects of postmodernism is the critique of the idea of *presence*, a concept that is fundamental to the modern concept of the subject. Presences refers to an idea of immediate experience, the direct understanding of the world through one's senses and perceptions as both reliable and real. Postmodernism says that this idea of presence, or immediate experience, is a myth, and that everything we experience is mediated through language, images, social forces, etc. In other words, postmodernism asserts that there is no such thing as pure, unmediated experience. The work of postmodern theory has been to examine these aspects of the postmodern condition and to make sense of the complexity of contemporary social interaction, meaning and cultural production. This does not mean that all aspects of contemporary societies are postmodern, rather that they work in tension with modern aspects and other influences."

2. ibid, Quote reproduced with permission of the Licensor through PLSclear. p. 252

3. "Postmodern undermines the epistemologies of depth that stood behind traditional representation; the manifest does not refer back to the latent, existence does not refer back to essence, signifier does not refer back to signified. So the only objects that could represent the world of surface would be precisely those that do not allow traditional representation. Put otherwise, postmodern could only be represented by objects that challenge representation itself." Turkle, Sherry, *Life On The Screen*, p. 275-footnote #10

4. Stuken, Marita, Cartwright, Lisa, *Practices of Looking*, relays postmodernism's short-sightedness (p. 258). Quote reproduced with permission of the Licensor through PLSclear. "Postmodern theory sees the surface as the primary element of social life, as opposed to the idea that the true meaning is hidden under-

neath. According to Baudrillard, the surface is all we see and all we can have access to. The image transcends the idea of the real, taking on a new importance in millennial culture. We can no longer look below the surface for depth and true meaning, because we will find nothing there."

5. Montag, Warren, "What is at Stake in the Debate on Postmodernism," in *Postmodernism and Its Discontents,* ed E. A. Kaplan, (p. 98) "Thus, an absolute determination (culture as expression) simplified to the greatest degree converges with a dubious knowledge that consists solely in the despairing recognition that the postmodern work of art is in fact unknowable . . . The work of art once full of meaning and affect and processed of a depth that seemed infinite has now become empty, alien and cold, no longer a representation of reality but a simulacrum of the simulacrum, a false representation of what is itself false."

6. Gibbs, Jr., William W., *Intentions in the Experience of Meaning,* I summarize these principles/methods from this book.

7. I like a statement by neurophysiologist Laura Sewell, "A superficial take on depth arises from superficial experience." Taken from *Sight and Sensibility,* p.164

8. The associative categories that interpret critical theory were taken from *Text and Contexts: Writing about Literature and Critical Theory,* by Steven Lynn.

9. Sanford, John and Paula, *The Elijah Task,* p. 214 Commenting on John 12:28-29.

10. When interpreting Biblical metaphors, as well as other Biblical figurative language, most people have an either/or approach; it is either literally true or it is a metaphor. God is bigger than each method. I have come to see metaphors may be metaphorically true and at times literally true. For example, light has been used as a metaphor many places in the Bible. As science has uncovered more of light's nature and our understanding of light has developed, we can no longer say a truth principle that uses light as a metaphor is *only* a metaphor; we recognize it may also be literally true in light of the expanded understanding of light's nature. So, figurative language may at times be an "and" instead of "either/or."

11. Schaeffer, Francis, *Art and the Bible,* p. 37. "...the artist makes a body of work, and this body shows his world view. No one, for example, who understands Michelangelo or Leonardo can look at their work without understanding something of their respective world views. Nonetheless, these artists began by making works of art, and then their world views showed through the body of their work. I emphasize the body of the artist's work because it is impossible for any single painting, for example, to reflect the totality of an artist's view of reality. But when we see a collection of an artist's paintings or a series of a poet's poems or a number of a novelist's novels, both the outline and some of the details of the artist's conception of life shine through."

12. The Hebrew words for judge:
    don—to remain
    šāpaṭ—to judge, decide; lead, defend, vindicate; to execute judgment, be brought to trial; to argue a matter
    mišpāṭ—justice, judgment; law, regulation, prescription
    diynāyē'—a judge. (found in Ezra 4:9)

A sampling of verses in Psalms which use judging:

Psalms 7:8 The Lord judges (*don*) the peoples; judge (*šāpaṭ*) me, O Lord according to my righteousness and according to the integrity that is in me.

Psalms 119:84 How long must your servant endure? When will you judge (*mišpāṭ*) those who persecute me?

13. With the Greek words for judging, here are a couple other verses to consider: 1 Corinthians 2:15 The spiritual person judges (*anakrinō*) all things, but is himself to be judged (*anakrinō*) by no one.

1 Corinthians 11:31 But if we judge (*diakrinō*) ourselves truly, we would not be judged (*krinō*)

James 2:12 So speak and so act as those who are to be judged (*krinō*) under the law of liberty.

14. Hebrew words for test:

bāthan—to test, try, probe, examine; to be tested, to test and learn the genuineness of an object

nāsāh—to test (usually to prove character or faithfulness), prove, test, try; to attempt to try God implies a lack of confidence in his revealed character and thus is wicked

sārap—to smelt, refine (metals), test

peh—mouth (human or animal); by extension speech, command, testimony; any opening; edge (of a sword); edge; mouth; opening. In Proverbs 27:2, The crucible is for silver, and the furnace is for gold, and a man is tested (*peh*) by his praise.

The Psalms give a good overview of the Hebrew words for testing:

Psalms 11:5 The Lord tests (*bāthan*) the righteous...

Psalms 26:2 Prove (*bāthan*) me, O Lord, and try (*nāsāh*) me; test (*sārap*) my heart and my mind.

Jeremiah 17:10 I the Lord search the heart and test (*bāthan*) the mind, to give every man according to his ways, according to the fruit of his deeds."

15. Here are a couple other verses to ponder on testing: Galatians 6:4 But let each one test (*dokimazō*) his own work, and then the reason to boast will be in himself alone and not in his neighbor.

James 1:3 For you know the testing (*dokimion*) of your faith produces steadfastness.

16. Santayana, George, *The Sense of Beauty*, p.16

17. *Anima* (Latin)-soul, life, *zōē* (Greek)-life, motion, activity; *hay* (Hebrew)-life, state of living (in contrast to death), lifetime. These words describe the motion or activity of life.

18. Siren, Osvald, *The Chinese on the Art of Painting*, p.20-21. The principles of painting were formulated by Hsieh Ho in the fifth century, called the Six Principles or Six Classics. The Six Principles became the accepted foundational doctrines of Chinese art.

1) ch'i-yun sheng-tung—Spirit Resonance (or vibration of vitality) and Life Movement.

2) Structural Brush-work.

3) Conform the objects in order of their likeness.

The objects of nature, the figures, flowers, animals, or whatever motifs that might be chosen, were never to the Chinese simply decorative forms or appearances, they always carried meaning, a spirit which had to be expressed through the forms. There is a symbolism not of intellect but an aesthetic or spiritual kind; its form is never constant.

4) Apply the Colors according to the Characteristics.

5) Plan and Design, Place and Position (i.e. composition).

6) Transmit Models by Drawing." Students copy Older models, which is the traditional path of learning.

These principles may be found in almost any book about Chinese paintings.

4

KINGDOM THINKING WITH ART

You are the salt of the earth, but if salt has lost its taste, how shall its saltiness be restored? It is no longer good for anything except to be thrown out and trampled under people's feet. You are the light of the world. A city set on a hill cannot be hidden. Nor do people light a lamp and put it under a basket, but on a stand, and it gives light to all in the house. In the same way, let your light shine before others, so that they may see your good works and give glory to your Father who is in heaven.

Matthew 5:13-16

Imagine you are sitting on a hill formed as a mini amphitheater, looking down toward Jesus, as he delivers the Sermon on the Mount. You heard Jesus say, "You are the salt of the earth." What do you suppose he means? Are we to evangelize? Do we make sure we always present the "right" message?

Jesus used two metaphors in this section of the Sermon on the Mount. The first, as just mentioned, is salt; next is light. Both metaphors give a picture of the influence we have. Let us try to get a clearer idea of Jesus' meaning so we may effectively interact with the people who live in the *Land of the Arts*.

SALT

Jesus presented salt with a strong warning:

> *You are the salt of the earth, but if salt has lost its taste, how shall its saltiness be restored? It is no longer good for anything except to be thrown out and trampled under people's feet.*

Matthew 5:13

Bible teachers and scholars have expounded on salt's usage in ancient times. Salt is seasoning, to influence and bring out flavors in the food where sprinkled. Salt was also a preservative, was used for medicinal purposes, as a cleaning agent, and to sterilize an enemy's land.[1]

Many of the biblical teachings on being salt relay the seasoning characteristic, which affect everything it touches. If we are "the salt of the earth," what does this mean? We will skim through some art history to show the impact of the Church's "salting" in the Visual arts, Music, Literature, and Dance. Works of art provide a tangible record of the influence of ideas on society.

VISUAL ART

In the Acts of the Apostles, persecution drove believers in Jesus Christ out of Jerusalem to disperse into the Roman Empire. The scattered believers preached the gospel of the kingdom every place they traveled, made disciples, and gathered them into groups. Because of their effectiveness in sharing the gospel of the kingdom, increased cruelty against believers, now called Christians, arose across the Roman Empire. Intensified persecution caused Christians to meet in secret. One place they covertly gathered was in the catacombs and tombs underneath the city of Rome (between 100 and 380+ AD). Christian-themed murals have been found in the ancient catacomb meeting places.

In 380 AD, when Christianity became the official religion throughout the Roman Empire, Christians met openly and built churches. The explosion in church buildings and cathedrals swept through Romanized Europe, North Africa, the Middle East, and through the Byzantine Empire to Russia and China, eventually spreading throughout Africa, the Americas, Australia, and the rest of the world. The church building boom has lasted for 1700+ years.

Sculpture was incorporated as ornamentation in churches and as a teaching aid for illiterate congregations. Mosaics and paintings were also used for decoration and teaching aids. Priests added other objects to churches through the centuries, such as icons and stained-glass windows. Through the Dark Ages and the Middle Ages, sculptures, paintings, and stained-glass windows transmitted the doctrines of the Church: depicting the birth, life, death, and resurrection of Christ; Old Testament stories; Jesus' parables; stories of the Apostles and the New Testament; the Apocalypse and Last Judgment, themes of Hell and Paradise; as well as Apocryphal legends/stories—of the Old and New Testaments, of Mary and the Saints.[2]

In medieval society, artists were not independent thinkers but artisans interpreting the subjects according to the priest's directions.[3] To simplify what society was like in the Dark and Middle Ages, it centered on community and each person's confined class and role restrictions. Art expressed the Medieval societal cultural view. A couple of works that exemplify this are: the surviving *Books of Hours* from the Middle Ages, and Renaissance Flemish artist Pieter Bruegel the Elder's (1525-1569) depictions of peasant life.

Various factors arose in the Renaissance to change society's focal points towards the individual. Historian Walter Sorell summarized this transition, "Renaissance man rediscovered the *humanness* in himself."[4] Sorell described the view artists held towards the arts, as they rediscovered their humanity: "Nature was seen in a different light, and through its close study the artist reached out to the expression of an ideal beauty. Curiosity led to experiments, and experiments led to knowledge, which gave man a feeling of totality."[5]

The Renaissance's expanded thinking was facilitated by the Fourteenth century's concentration of artistic geniuses, such as Giotto, Leonardo da Vinci, Michelangelo, Albrecht Durer, and many others. I could go into a developed summary of how these artists experimented with anatomy, proportions, perspective, light, color, sought greater pictorial naturalism, and even applied scientific observations to their studies of nature and the human body. Suffice it to say that many books already chronicle the Quattrocento Artists' development through their works, including their impact on society.

One trigger for Europe's transition was the Gutenberg printing press, invented in Germany around 1440. The printing press gave people the ability to acquire their own Bible and other books, which stimulated and hastened the separation away from communal roles. The procedure required to print on Gutenberg's press was not a quick activity. Carve the letter or image for illustration on the front of a woodblock, gather the block-letters into words and sentences, add the pictures—commissioned to artists —at the appropriate placement, apply ink over the raised areas of the letter blocks and illustration panels, and with the pressure of the printing press, transfer the inked image to paper. Finally, assemble the pages in order, and bind them together along with the cover.

When the "Revelation of John" was printed at the end of the 1400s, Albrecht Durer's (1471-1528 German) image of the *Four Horsemen of the Apocalypse* (1497-1498) illustrated the sixth chapter of Revelation and is still its best-known depiction. With society shifting towards the individual, the public expanded their appreciation for more picture subjects. The Renaissance increased interests for portraits, landscapes, still lifes, city scenes.

MUSIC

Jesus, during his last Passover supper, sang with his disciples the designated psalms for Passover. All Jews knew the Psalms, and believers in Christ continued the tradition of singing Psalms as they gathered. Saint Paul, in his letter to the Ephesians, exhorted them to "speak to one another in psalms and hymns and spiritual songs, singing and making melody to the Lord with your hearts, giving thanks always..." (Ephesians 5:19). This verse infers that the early Church sang psalms, hymns, and spiritual songs, presumably composed by talented individuals in the congregations. The early Church used instruments during their gatherings, at least for a while. Scripture abundantly mentions music, so the early Church Fathers supported its benefit in spiritual discipline.[6] But the early Church Fathers were cautious of music's negative influence, as the Greek Theater exerted a powerful influence on the culture,[7] including musical instruments being associated with pagan worship. The caution of the early Church Fathers towards instruments meant eventually instrument usage in gatherings declined.[8]

Christian monasteries were established in the fourth century.[9] During each of the nine services held per day, monks chanted in Latin the psalms a cappella. Chanting occurred one of two ways: as *responsive* or as an *antiphony* (against sound). The responsive method entails a call and response, where a leader's voice gives a verse, and the congregation joins with the refrain. Antiphony is where two or more voices alternate and contrast with each other.[10]

Plain chant was the singing form the Church used at the time monasteries started. The antiphony form formed in the monasteries, and by the fifth century, the Church adopted its use in the Mass.[11] The Gregorian Chant developed from plain chant and contains both responsive and antiphony forms. Gregorian Chants include psalmodies chants, where Psalms are sung without refrains to uncomplicated tones, and may contain responsive and antiphony uses.[12] I speculate the monks or nuns intoning and harmonizing the Latinized psalms in unison during Mass created an inviting atmosphere for the Holy Spirit's joyful habitation to their praises, which electrified the atmosphere.

Let us look at an example of the basic response approach. A leader or cantor would sing the first part of a verse, and the congregation would respond with the next part. Psalm 136 has at the end of each verse, the line, "For His mercy endures forever"; the cantor chants the verse, then the congregation replies, "For His mercy endures forever."[13] Along this approach, two choirs may use call and response to sing the Psalms.

In the 8th and 9th centuries, the organ added another element to the way congregations sang the Psalms.[14] Through later centuries, the organ took on its own voice and place in public worship. In 1527, St. Mark's Church in Venice hired Adrian Willaert from Flanders to become the organ master. When he arrived, he found two organs facing each other across the aisle. This likely inspired him to have two choirs, which the Venetians delighted in and called "liquid gold".[15] Willaert's approach inspired other composers to write for two, three, and even four choirs. Over time, churches added other instruments, replacing the sound of multiple choirs with the instruments' sounds. In due course, musical instruments presented a composer's songs without the human voice, called a concerto (from the Latin word *concertare*, meaning to contest or rival).[16] From this approach, the symphony concert originated out of the Church.

The Psalms inspired many, many Christian composers through the ages to formulate their praise to God. Few songs have survived. One enduring hymn is *Be Thou My Vision*, from an Old Irish text attributed to Saint Dallan Forgaill in the sixth century, though a few scholars attribute it to the eighth century. This Plain Chant hymn became part of the Irish monastic tradition. In 1905, Mary Elizabeth Byrne translated the text into English and Eleanor Hull versified it in 1912, into the form we are familiar with today.[17]

Another enduring hymn is *All Creatures of Our God and King,* written by Saint Francis of Assisi, circa 1224. Saint Francis' text became known as *Cantico di fratre sole* (Song of Brother Sun), also called the Canticle of the Sun. Around 1911, William H. Draper translated Saint Francis' song to English, but he paraphrased it, and added the title: "All Creatures of Our God and King." Experts credit the tune as a seventeenth-century German folk melody.[18]

At the end of the Middle Ages, as focus moved toward the individual, society placed greater obligation on personal responsibility. Martin Luther was a man of his times, his development as a Catholic priest and his study of Scripture reinforced responsibility to God and others. Luther translated the Bible into the common language of German, so ordinary people might read the Scriptures. He wrote hymns in German instead of Latin, so that people could sing songs to God in their own language, without the barrier of a High Language. Luther wrote the lyrics and melodies to songs, like *A Mighty Fortress is our God* (1527-1529).[19] Sometimes he based melodies on familiar folk tunes, maybe even used beer hall melodies, which a few scholars doubt, though I accept as a probable source. Hymn writers since, such as Isaac Watts and Charles Wesley, wrote songs using Scriptures or paraphrases of Scripture expressed through their common language.

Gutenberg's press allowed a composer's music to disseminate beyond the immediate concert. Many composers whom we classify as Classical wrote music to God, for church use and for the general society. Bach and Handel are the best-known today. Incidentally, Bach's influence on music was so deep and impactful, music developed into the form we are now familiar with; labeled "modern".

Jumping forward in time, another category we will touch on is American Spirituals. Black slaves sang these songs on plantations since the early days of the American South. Suffering underlies most American Spirituals, while looking in hope to God. The beauty of hope is why these songs continue to inspire.

In the 1960s, churches transitioned from a congregation singing hymns to choruses. The change was a partial reaction to a 1960s-1970s cultural/generational divide, in which hymns were associated with an old approach and choruses were also becoming the stylistic preference of the time. The choruses of the 1960s-1970s often used unaltered Scripture verses put to music. Today, we no longer sing straight Scripture verses. Most of the chorus songs today place the subject's weight on personal identification and feelings, though God may be mentioned: i.e., God loves me, I am forgiven, God makes me happy, I am remembered, I want God more, The result of "me-centered" songs, they propagate a soul-centered perspective.[20] Consequently, many worship songs we sing espouse unscriptural theology. For more on this subject, you can refer to Chapter Six.

LITERATURE

We inherit the love of Scripture from the priests and rabbis who stewarded the Scriptures since Moses. The Apostles' letters, as we read in Acts, were hand-copied, and passed around among the first century churches, then later, recognized as part of the Christian Scriptures. Monks took up the duties of hand-copying the Scriptures. Over time, monks added calligraphic flourishes, such as the first letter of a page being larger than the rest of the text. Then developed into adding decorative borders and motifs to the Scriptural texts, with many surviving examples from Ireland. As a side note, Irish monks, during the Dark Ages, preserved Scriptures from destruction, saving them from the overwhelming Barbarian hordes.

After the 1440s, Gutenberg's printing press made possible the mass production of the Scriptures, which made the Bible available for common people instead of only for the clergy and nobility. Throughout history, Christians wrote books that shaped societal views. Here is a list of a few: St. Augustine's *Autobiography* (401 AD) and *City of God* (426), St. Thomas Aquinas' *Summa Theo-*

logica (1265-1274), Dante's *Divine Comedy* (1320), Martin Luther's *Ninety-Five Theses* (1517), John Foxe's *Foxe's Book of Martyrs* (1560), John Bunyan's *Pilgrim's Progress* (1678). We could list an abundance of Christian writings to the present time touching on theology, philosophy, history, and fiction.

One other subject of literature worthy of mention is the history of indigenous cultures written by missionaries and priests that went to those cultures. They preserved the histories of Ireland, Mexico, many cultures in the Americas, Africa, Asia, Australia, and islands of the Pacific.

To summarize, most Christian written works sought to shed light on or expound upon Scriptural truth, even when Scriptural truth was not followed in society or in the Church. Some of these works shaped the times, cultures, and societies in which they were written. Many shaped generations since.

DANCE

Now, let us touch on the often neglected subject of Dance. As with Music, the Church in the first century distanced itself from Dance and its idolatrous associations, especially the Dionysian ecstatic frenzy.

Guttenberg's printing press allowed books on dance to be distributed to the public.

French theologians wrote about dance during the Baroque Age. Father Marin Mersenne (1588-1648) was a mathematician and philosopher whose important work was *Harmonie Universelle*, full of searching thoughts about music, dance, and life. "For Father Mersenne, the 'principle end' of all art 'was to delight the cultivated listener, and not to rouse his passions.'"[21] In 1658, the Abbé Michel de Pure wrote in his *Idée des Spectacles* a dictum that expressed an underlying belief prevalent to this day: *le sujet est l'âme du ballet,* meaning the subject (a soloist dancer who graduated above the corps but not yet to premier dancer[22]) is the soul of the ballet. But he must have envisioned ballet as a far more independent art form, since he referred to it as an "expressive pantomime," believing that it could represent through gestures and movements "that which could be expressed by words." "His ideas were formulated three years before the French academy for dancing, L'Académie Royale de Danse, was founded in Paris. He helped prepare the right ambience for it by siding with the professionals against the noblemen, who, he felt, participated in ballets for the sake of 'vanity and personal interest.' He expected the dance master to make a clear distinction between the social dance and ballet as a new art form."[23] The Abbé Jean-Baptiste du Bos (1670-1742) described dance as an "animated and mobile painting."[24] Abbé du Bos, also, spoke of dance as *"le langage du coeur,"* he felt that in expressive movement lies the secret of being and becoming.[25]

These theologians observed the creative aspects of movement and dance, and wrote about the artform because they understood its role of influence in society. "They also may, in an age and world torn by religious strife, have looked for a unifying gesture that *one* God gave to all of us: movement and the ability to make people move to their heart's delight and by the will of their minds."[26]

MOVING AWAY FROM THE ARTS

I identify the impetus of the Counter-Reformation[27] as the start of the Church's gradual departure from the arts. The Church restricted "salting" since the Edict of Worms (1521) from the Catholic Church's reaction to Luther and other reformers.[28] Concurrent with the Council of Trent, the Catholic Church re-established the Inquisition in 1542, which is when I pinpoint the Church quit its "salting".[29] Both the Catholic and Protestant Church constrained the arts, forcing artists to follow popular cultural philosophies. Over the centuries artists stood alone, without support from the Church, though the Catholic Church validated artists more often than did the Protestant Church.

The effect through history of the Church's withdrawal from

living as the salt of the earth in the arts, we withheld the Gospel from seasoning culture. We also suppressed the preservative nature of being the salt of the earth, preventing and slowing down the decay of sin. When the Church quit seasoning cultural grounds, whatever seeds the wind blew took root. Today's culture results from the Church's miserly salting, thus allowing the enemy to sow its own seeds and tend the cultural grounds.

Ironically, our collective memory of long ago when the Church supported the arts and tended the culture has stopped us from plowing up today's ground. The excuse given is that it is not like it was then. True! Those days are gone. Today is a fresh start. We can shape the arts as the Holy Spirit directs. We must let go of excuses and sprinkle the salt; because *agape* salting influences culture, even shapes cultural development. In this way, we fight the war for the arts.

LIGHT

Having examined Jesus' metaphor of salt in relation to the arts, we come to Jesus' next metaphor: Light.

You are the light of the world. A city set on a hill cannot be hidden. Nor do people light a lamp and put it under a basket, but on a stand, and it gives light to all the house. In the same way, let your light shine before others, so that they may see your good works and give glory to your Father who is in heaven.

Matthew 5:14-16

I first learned about light in my seventh grade art class, where we studied the effects of light by drawing a white ball on a piece of white paper, with one light source about three feet away, pointed downward at a 45-degree angle, casting a shadow onto the paper. In the first class, the teacher completely covered the windows, shut off the overhead lights in the room, and turned on a lamp directed at the ball; then he demonstrated how to draw the ball. In the next class, we students drew the ball, which was again lit up in the darkened classroom. We continued working on this drawing of the ball every day for a week. Then we started a new drawing, where the teacher added an object to the setup. Each week was a new drawing with added objects. We learned what light does when encountering one object, then two, and three, and more. We drew several bones of a cow, then a cow skull under the light of the lamp. The skull drawing prepared us to draw ourselves in the mirror by observing the light and shadow of those structures, showing us the way light falls over our faces.

When I teach beginning drawing—to people 9 years old through age 80—I employ this same approach, so as students draw the ball, they discover how light bends and bounces. Through this method, students learn to actually see what they observe, while letting go of what they think the setup is about. Through drawing light and shadows, I discovered what Jesus meant when He said, "you are the light of the world". I learned how much one light source illuminates a darkened room, how light affects darkness, and how light bends and bounces around as it interacts with different object-forms and materials. Many Christian adults I taught in this beginning class experienced a dramatic revelation about light.

SACRED AND SECULAR

Jesus said that in the last days, the love of many will grow cold because lawlessness will increase (Matthew 24:12). The Church's withdrawal from many sectors of society happened because its love cooled. When love cools, we do less salting and restrict our light. In so doing, we categorize areas of life as either sacred or secular. The beginnings of this intellectual separation reaches as far back as Adam and Eve's departure from Eden. The full development of thinking is expressed in Greek Neo-Platonism and Gnostic thought. The early Church fought against these beliefs as heresy. Yet many Christians today judge life through a sacred/secular filter, where the sacred is viewed as morally correct, and the products in the secular arena are neutral at best, immoral at worst.

The sacred/secular view held by Christians can allow con men to deceive them because a sacred label covers the swindle. Or, they miss divine inspiration upon something not labeled as sacred. Christians deceived by a sacred/secular perspective will pass on their judgments about people and their works, because they have not learned to test a person's words and works. Jesus addressed this sacred/secular double-mindedness when he ate at Zacchaeus' house in Luke 19:1-10. Zacchaeus, the chief tax collector, worked for the Roman overlords. Israel viewed tax collectors as traitors, and the religious rulers grumbled because Jesus went to a sinner's house. Those who hold a sacred/secular viewpoint assume everything not sacred is contaminating, so we must keep away from whatever will foul us up. If people with a sacred/secular perspective met Zacchaeus today, would they tell him that he should quit working for the Roman heathens so they would not defile him? Jesus did not say this. The sacred/secular view means light is not for the world but restricted to a sacred box, to one location, at certain times, or for only certain people. In verse 10, Jesus answered the Pharisees' sacred/secular grumblings: "The Son of Man came to seek and save the lost". This is Jesus' answer to the sacred/secular worldview. The effect of a dualistic view of life is that we withdraw from touching whatever is not sacred, because it is outside, impure, either for/from God or for/from the Devil. We do not want worldly pursuits or products or people to contaminate us.

One movie that shows how the dualism of secular and sacred negatively affects creative people is *St. Louis Blues* (1958), starring Nat King Cole, Eartha Kitt, Pearl Bailey, Ella Fitzgerald, and Cab Calloway. *St. Louis Blues* is broadly based on the life of musician and composer W. C. Handy (1873-1958), known as the father of The Blues. The movie depicts him growing up in Memphis, with a strict widower preacher-father and his aunt. Being raised in church, his father told him many times that music was for the Lord or for the Devil. Someone outside of church recognized Handy's talent and asked him to write a song for a local politician's rally, which introduced to him the idea that music could go beyond the church walls. His growing interest in the music of the street tore him from the music of the church, driving a wedge of conflict between his father and him. As he published his songs, his relationship with his father became more strained. Then he lost his eyesight and had to move back home. He wrote church hymns during that time, and his eyesight returned. Soon, the conflict between church music and street music returned, accompanied by renewed conflict with his father. He left home to tour the United States, expanding his repertoire and audience. At the end of the movie, a symphony orchestra plays Handy's music, recognizing him as the father of America's first authentic art form, The Blues. Handy's father was persuaded to come to the concert, to witness the impact of his son's music. In the end, father and son were reconciled.

What I find interesting in the story of *St. Louis Blues,* is how the movie makers depicted Christians' judgmental interactions towards creativity and its outlets. Today, a lot of Christians hold the same judgmental views towards the arts, as being only either for God or for the Devil.

German theologian Dietrich Bonhoeffer (1906-1945) has a contrary view.

> The Christian's task is to live out life in terms of his secular calling. This is the way to die unto the world. The value of the secular calling for Christians is that it provides an opportunity of living the Christian life with the support of God's grace, and engaging more vigorously in the assault on the world and everything it stands for... By recalling the Christians into the world, he called them paradoxically out of it more. That is what Luther experienced in his own person. His call to men to return

to the world was essentially a call to enter the visible Church of the incarnate God.[30]

Bonhoeffer saw a higher sacred calling in living as a Christian, in the darkness of a secular world. How do we do this, or in what way should we approach it? We apply the Kingdom of God to each area of our lives. Then, as ambassadors of God's Kingdom, we represent him, showing others how to live a life through Jesus' divine love and life.

Jesus taught that the Kingdom of God/Heaven is here at hand. Most of Jesus's parables are about the Kingdom of God, which opposes a division of sacred and secular. Jesus completes his teaching on light by saying, "In the same way [having a light out in the open], let your light shine before others, so that they may see your good works and give glory to your Father who is in heaven" (Matthew 5:16). Jesus tells us to shine "this little light of mine" all around. The way we shine light to and through the arts is to get involved, as creative people and as the audience. Without involvement, our light stays hidden, and the lost remain in the dark. When Jesus said to shine our light before others, he added, "**so that they** (those to whom you shine your light in your area of influence) **may see your good works.**" Is the reason we withhold shining our light because our works are not good, or because we are afraid that the secular will pollute us? Maybe we judge that "those dirty sinners" will contaminate God's kingdom if we bring our good works in their midst.

THE KINGDOM OF GOD IS NEAR

If (and for many, this is a big if) we are to be Christ's witnesses, as Acts 1 says, what do we bear witness about? First, what God has done in our life is a good start. And like Jesus, you bring the Kingdom of God with you because you are its representative, an ambassador.[31] Christ in you, the hope of glory, is wherever you are. Through you, God's love extends to the lost.

Jesus considered the Kingdom of Heaven important. It is the first topic he preached in Matthew 4:17. Jesus taught the gospel of the kingdom throughout his ministry; it featured in parables to the crowds, training his disciples, and through demonstrations of power with miracles, healing the sick, and casting out demons. We also are to represent God's kingdom, as Jesus did, which shapes our entire life and our creative expressions.

How should we regard life through a Kingdom of God lens?[32] I want to emphasize that how we perceive the Kingdom of God influences our creative expressions to others. Jesus' parable of the talents, in Matthew 25:14-30, is how we will reflect on this question. First, let us view the context in which Jesus framed the parable of the talents.

Jesus began his thought in Matthew 24, talking about how no one knows when the Father is returning (vs. 36). Jesus gives several examples and says in vs. 44, "Therefore you also must be ready, for the Son of Man is coming at an hour you do not expect." Then Jesus asked in vs. 45, "Who is the faithful and wise servant the master has set over his household...?" With this question in mind, Jesus tells the parable of ten virgins (Matt. 25:1-13), who waited for the bridegroom to return. The bridegroom delayed and did not arrive until a late hour. Half of the virgins let their lamp oil run out, then left to refill the oil. After they left, the bridegroom arrived and took the virgins whose lamps were ready for the marriage celebration. Entrance was refused to the virgins who were unprepared.

Next, Jesus gives the story of talents (Matthew 25:14-30), which we will look at closely in the next section,[33] followed by the parable of the sheep and the goats (Matthew 25:31-46). In this parable, the Son of Man comes in glory, with the angels, to judge the people. He separates people into two groups. One group called "sheep," who were placed on the right hand, will "inherit the kingdom, prepared for them from the foundation of the world". The other group called "goats," are placed on the left, will be thrown into "eternal fire prepared for the devil and his angels".

What distinguishes the sheep from goats, according to this parable, is that one group gave food to the hungry, drink to the thirsty, welcomed strangers, clothed the naked, visited the sick, and visited prisoners; in other words, they helped those in need. The other group did not.

PARABLE OF TALENTS

Within the framework of these parables, let us examine the parable of the talents and apply it to the arts. I will paraphrase the first half of the story, because it is long.

> A man readying to go on a journey called his servants and entrusted to them his possessions. To one servant he gave five talents, to another, two talents, and to another one talent, each according to their ability. Then he went away. The one with five talents went at once and traded with them and made five more. Also, the one with two talents made two more. The servant who received one talent dug a hole and hid it. After a long time away, the master returned and called together his servants.
>
> The one who received five talents brought forth ten talents, saying, "Master, you delivered to me five talents. Here I made five talents more." The master replied, "Well done my good and faithful servant. You have been faithful over little; I will set you over much. Enter into the joy of your master." The one who had been given two talents brought out four talents, saying, "Master, you delivered to me two talents; here, I made two talents more." The master replied, "Well done my good and faithful servant. You have been faithful over little; I will set you over much. Enter into the joy of your master." The one who received one talent came forward, saying, "Master, I knew you to be a hard man, reaping where you do not sow, and gathering where you scattered no seed. I was afraid and hid your talent in the ground. Here is the talent back that you gave me." The

master answered, "You wicked and slothful servant! You knew I reap where I did not sow and gather where I scattered no seeds. You should have invested the money with bankers, and when I returned, I would have received the talent with its interest. So, take the talent from him and give it to the one with ten talents. For to everyone who has more will be given, and he will have in abundance. But from the one who has not, even what he has will be taken away. And now cast the worthless servant into outer darkness. In that place there will be weeping and gnashing of teeth." (Summary of Matthew 25:14-30)

A talent in Jesus' culture was coinage; money. In our culture, the word "talent" has come to mean ability, both natural and learned. Talent is a term often used when referring to people making works of art, in any form. With either view, a talent is useless if not used. Both the servant with five talents and the servant with two talents developed and increased the talents they received. The servant given one talent did not cultivate it; through his fear, he wrapped his talent and entombed it. Buried talents are actively suppressed and hidden; potential unrealized. To use monetary terms regarding our God-given abilities, there is no gain on God's investment in us when we bury our talents.

At the beginning of the parable, the master entrusted his possessions to the servants before he left. The Greek word used for possessions is *hyparchō*, which means to begin, to come into existence; to exist; to be, subsist; to be in possession, to belong; goods, possession, property. The master did not just give his servants money, but gave them a part of his existence, his being revealed through physical goods. The servants increasing the master's physical goods, showed that they may faithfully steward more signs of his being; in essence, they may be trusted with his life. The wicked servant showed he was untrustworthy with the master's life because he buried that part of the master's existence given to him.

When the Church withdrew from life outside the walls of the

church building, hiding its gifts and talents in its wrappings, which servant did it imitate? Because God is merciful, he delays returning that we might prepare as the wise virgins. Remember, God issued to us talent-abilities. My art background taught me that *all* talent must be developed. Over the years, I met several "talented" high school artists. I heard some of them talk in a way that betrayed an assumption they learned everything needed, instead of realizing their ability is just a beginner. Talent is only as good as the way we exercise it, and if we don't use what ability we have, it will dry up.

The question we must answer for ourselves is, "How will I use my abilities and for whom?" We find the answer in the parable of the sheep and goats, about who met the needs of people in the world. Our talents are the avenue to people's situations, where God's life in us, the hope of glory, directs us to their need, maybe even touching the unvoiced longing of their heart. When we use our talents and abilities, we share the Master's life realized through our works. This is part of the answer to the question several pages back, about how to "regard life through the kingdom of God lens".

GOD'S KINGDOM IS ACTIVE

Our society has returned to a pagan hedonism found in the book of Acts. Paul's description in Romans 1 is a good summation of society's present outlook.

> *...they became futile in their thinking, and their foolish hearts were darkened. And since they did not see fit to acknowledge God, God gave them up to a debased mind, to do what ought not to be done. They were filled with all manner of unrighteousness, evil, covetousness, malice...*

> Romans 1:28-29

We have come full circle. These verses bring us back to the present. Futile reasoning increases in people's hearts in proportion to the reduced level of light in society. So, what are we going to do about it? Stay in our buildings, waiting for someone to check on us? Or have we regulated our living so life outside the church walls will not contaminate us? Is this how the Kingdom of God functions?

The Kingdom of God is active, not passive; seasoning where sprinkled; dissipating darkness with light. God's Kingdom goes to the needy, to care, to heal, and to deliver; affecting every area its representatives are at. Even the arts.

When we view life through the Kingdom of God lens, we connect to every area of life. This raises the question, "In what way should we involve ourselves as we engage in life's creative areas?" We involve ourselves as maker-participants and as an engaged audience.

SUBJECT MATTER

If we become makers, toward whom should we target our works? It is good to be a Christian artist, directing works to a Christian audience. It is also good to be an artist who, as a Christian, makes works for everyone in the world.

Therefore, what is acceptable subject matter? This question stems from a sacred/secular mindset, which is a hindrance to living in a Kingdom mindset. All areas of life are in God's Kingdom. We may address every subject as the Holy Spirit brings it into focus. The whole of life, positive and negative, may be used in the arts.

When we are an audience, a Kingdom of God understanding informs how we engage any works we encounter. As we behold the works of art in front of us, we can perceive, interact with, and even enjoy the art pertaining to every area of life, inside or outside a Christian context.

HOLD FAST TO THE GOOD

In the last chapter, 1 Thessalonians 5:21 says to, "Test all things and hold fast to what is good." This verse is a good summation of aesthetics but is hard to carry out because we rarely discern the good. To take part in the arts as composer/presenter, we are to make works that withstands *every* test—compositionally, aesthetically, content-wise, etc. If we are to be an informed audience, we must recognize how to test creative endeavors. When testing works, we examine *how* a Content is Expressed, but without our habit of moral judging, all the while verifying if the work has a spark of life.

A good example of the fallout of our moral judgments is the incident I described in the Introduction, with the person who looked through my notebook. The person's judgmental actions killed the relationship I had with the family, and their words and actions poisoned how I was perceived. The person placed theirself as judge, separated and condemned me in the trail of their mind, then voiced their judgment. They unwittingly repeated the enemy's condemnations. I had to forgive the person many, many times; then I put the offense and anger over the injustice done to me on the cross to die. I nailed their judgments about me and my judgments of them on the cross, then applied to my life Romans 8:1, "There is therefore now no condemnation for those who are in Christ Jesus."

When we apply morality to how we consider art, we judge the surface perception of a work with how we identify right and wrong. Is there a right or wrong subject or style? Is Art's rightness "correct" only when sacred? The answer is no. Many Christians make bad art, despite good motives. A message with a good intention does not determine its correctness or "goodness". In fact, good and bad are not the same as right and wrong. Some people may have thoughts flash through their mind in response to these statements: "What about nudity? Do you advocate promiscuity? Should we accept everything that contaminates us, like how dancing encourages us to release sexual urges or listening to country music encourages us to drink and cheat?"

Jesus responded to the Pharisees' sacred/secular outlook; exclaiming to them:

> *Woe to you, scribes and Pharisees, hypocrites! For you clean the outside of the cup and plate, but inside they are full of greed and self-indulgence. You blind Pharisees! First clean the inside of the cup and the plate, that the outside also may be clean.*
>
> *Woe to you, scribes and Pharisees, hypocrites! For you are like whitewashed tombs, which outwardly appear beautiful, but within are full of dead people's bones and all uncleanness. So you also outwardly appear righteous to others, but within you are full of hypocrisy and lawlessness.*

Matthew 23:25-28

Something outside of us will **not** *make us* sin. Nudity can be a fascination because it is not a common sight. Frankly, most people should *not* be naked. Are you aware God told a prophet or two to go around naked for a time? God told Isaiah to be naked as a sign to the people of Israel (Isaiah 20:2,3). You may reply that God would not say it today. But can you be sure? We presume he will not say it again. But who knows? Nakedness does not offend God, as we read in Genesis chapter two.

The actual issue is in the heart. If a person lacks self-control, they will act out whatever whim grabs them. Fearing the surrounding stimuli is one reason a person defaults to what I call, "*Footloose*'s Model of Judgment". To manage temptation, we make rules towards everything assumed to contaminate us. We also exert temptation management towards other people. The individuals who dictate *others'* motives and actions may dislike the responsibility of self-control, instead they hold others accountable for their own weaknesses. As the saying goes, "If one cannot control themself, they will try to control others." Is temptation bad because it exposes weakness? Temptation is not bad as it is a test, showing us *our* flaws, giving us a chance to strengthen the weak area or surrender the issue to God and receive his strength and resurrected life.

To answer the sacred/secular question about using subject matter like nudity: there are subjects in which the use of nudity in art is appropriate and others in which it is not. The same can be said regarding the use of language, even profanity, found in stories and songs. How do we know which treatment is suitable? We consider a work's idea, and *how* it is Expressed, which helps us to perceive people's works objectively. We do not have to approve a work to see it impartially.

A PRACTICAL EXAMPLE OF SALTING AND SHINING

Because the Kingdom of Heaven is a kingdom, it affects every area of life; therefore, we may address each aspect of life with salting and shining. We can sprinkle salt and shine more effectively when we assess if an Expression suits an idea's Content. Imagine being at a gallery, meeting an artist, and talking about their displayed pictures. Our familiar judgmental-moral condemnations erects barriers difficult to get around. Instead, talk about how successful or not a work is at conveying its idea. If the work does not express its idea well, discuss *how* the work may realize its potential. As we discuss the idea's successful presentation, any perceived moral issues might be discussed without shutting down an individual. In other words, we may form a relationship. Salt is sprinkled. Light shines. Perceptions may expand. We impart God's Life. Keep in mind when you are in these situations that *every* work, in *every* art form, is approached through the way the work Expresses a Content.

Let us return to the Scripture mentioned at the beginning of the chapter:

You are the salt of the earth, but if salt has lost its taste, how shall its saltiness be restored? It is no longer good for anything except to be thrown out and trampled under people's feet. You are the light of the world. A city set on a hill cannot be hidden.

Matthew 5:13-14

You *are* salt. You *are* light. You will affect people because you are there, even without speaking. And when you communicate, remember you are God's representative—ambassador of His agape and His life.

---

1. *The Zondervan Pictorial Bible Dictionary*, p. 742-743
2. Mâle, Emile, *The Gothic Image: Religious Art in France of the Thirteenth Century.* (Reproduced by permission of Taylor and Francis Group.) Mâle gives the various categories, showing how several cathedrals conveyed imagery depicting the themes and conveys in his book that the Apocryphal stories of Mary, the Apostles and Saints were taken from the Medieval book, *The Golden Legend* by Vincent of Beauvais.
3. ibid, p. 392-396 Mâle gives the Catholic Church's instruction concerning artists, set down during the Second Council of Nicea (787 AD), "The composition of religious imagery is not left to the initiative of artists, but is formed upon principles laid down by the Catholic Church and by religious tradition." And, "The execution alone belongs to the painter, the selection and arrangement of subject belongs to the Fathers."
4. Sorell, Walter, *Dance in its Time*, p. 46
5. ibid, p. 46
6. Routley, Erik, *The Church and Music*, I condensed and paraphrased a section from Chapter 2, under the heading "Music and the Early Church," p. 45-50.
7. ibid, p. 45-50
8. ibid, p. 50-55
9. ibid, p.71
10. Commins, Dorothy Berlinier, *All about the Symphony Orchestra: and What it Plays*, p. 82.
11. Summarized from Catholic Encyclopedia, under the category, Plain Chant; https://www.catholic.org/encyclopedia/view.php?id=9414
12. Summarized from Wikipedia; https://en.wikipedia.org/wiki/Gregorian_chant

13. Commins, Dorothy Berlinier, *All about the Symphony Orchestra: and What it Plays*, I use Commins' example of Psalms 136 to help understand the Responsive method, p. 82.

14. https://www.britannica.com/art/organ-musical-instrument

15. Commins, Dorothy Berliner, *All about the Symphony Orchestra: and What it Plays*, I summarized Adrian Willaert's story, p. 82-83

16. ibid, p. 83

17. Summarized from Wikipedia; https://en.wikipedia.org/wiki/Be_Thou_My_Vision

18. Summarized from Wikipedia; https://en.wikipedia.org/wiki/All_Creatures_of_Our_God_and_King

19. https://en.wikipedia.org/wiki/A_Mighty_Fortress_Is_Our_God

20. **A challenge** to music leaders in churches: for one month, sing songs without personal pronouns in them. Compare the dynamics and power during the worship time prior to and during the month of trying this. You will notice people engage more, the atmosphere will be more energized, and you will not have to "work up" the congregation.

21. Sorell, Walter, *Dance in It's Time*, p. 86

22. Chujoy, Anatole, *The Dance Encyclopedia*, p. 454, found in the section, "*Sujet.*"

23. Sorell, Walter, *Dance in It's Time*, p. 86-87

24. ibid, p.87. The Abbé Jean-Baptiste du Bos, in his *Réflexions Critiques sur la Poésie et la Peinture*, pointed to the ancient Greek dance as an expression that "had to signify something" in contrast to "the gestures of our dancers" which are "attitudes and movements that serve naught but gracefulness". His criticism moved, in the direction of the *ballet d'action*—ballet with a plot.

25. idid, p. 87

26. idid, p. 87

27. The Council of Trent met between 1545-1563, is classified as the official beginning of the Counter-Reformation or Catholic Reformation.

28. I use the term "reformer" for those like Luther, who did not originally intend to leave the Catholic Church, but wanted to raise issues to provoke the Church to move toward greater holiness, by letting go of the issues he perceived as barriers to its purity.

29. Goldwater, Robert, Treves, Marco, *Artists on Art, from the XIV to the XX Century*, p.103-108 Paulo Caliari, called Veronese, was examined by an Inquisition tribunal in 1573. The tribunal questioned a painting by Veronese of a last supper that Jesus Christ partook of with His Apostles in the house of Simon. The tribunal wanted him to take out or change many elements in the picture. Veronese did not change the picture but changed its title to *Supper in the House of Levi*.

30. Bonhoeffer, Dietrich, *The Cost of Discipleship*, p. 298

31. 2 Corinthians 5:20

32. Towards the end of Jesus delivering the Sermon on the Mount, he talked about the kingdom of God, saying, "Therefore do not be anxious, saying, 'What shall we eat?' or 'What shall we drink?' or 'What shall we wear?' For the Gentiles seek after all these things, and your heavenly Father knows that you need them

all. But seek first the kingdom of God and his righteousness, and all these things will be added to you." (Matthew 6:31-33)

33. Luke 19:12-27 gives a parallel but different version of a master going away while entrusting servants with ten, five, and one minas. A minas was a sixteenth part of a talent.

5

AUDIENCE

Once a maker concludes a work, everyone encountering it becomes its audience. We could state that a work is incomplete unless there are people to experience it.[1] An audience is central to the work's experience.

In this chapter, we will examine who we make works for. "Audience" is the term used for an individual or group experiencing a work. So, who is the audience? We can make something for ourselves, but primarily works are for other people. And when we become Christian, we may also address works to God.

Works made for ourselves are usually about self-expression. We may leave facets of the work undone or might not care about its balance and flow, because it is just for us. With such works, we rarely go beyond spouting utterances, to communicating ideas as an experience filled with vitality. Most of our works are for someone other than ourselves. A rough guess-timate is that 94 percent of everything people make falls into the category "for others".

Artists are nothing more than experts at experiencing. They have developed the skills to sustain and effectively apply their yearning, which enables them to notice well and engage productively with their own experience. And they also know how to make things that invite and guide the experience of others.[2]

Guiding others' experiences is a developed skill. When we make works for anyone other than ourselves, we must intentionally escort them through a work. Artists may include self-expression in their works, but self-expression alone does not lead others in their encounters. When makers conduct people through works, they must always keep in mind a couple questions. First, is the content engaging? Second, how are we rendering the theme? There are many factors that go into answering these questions.

Artists can tackle all topics of life, as the Holy Spirit brings an issue into focus in relation to his Word. An artist's works may show everything entailing life, love, the universe, and eternity; leading people to consider a subject through its presentation as an experience. A creator guides an audience according to how they combine a chosen medium's forms and elements in a compositional arrangement that best communicates the idea.

NOISE AND SKILL

King David seemed to understand when a work's purpose was for individual expression or for others, including God. He categorized the distinction with the terms: "noise" and "skill". He said in several psalms, to "make a joyful noise". Psalms 100:1 declares, "Make a joyful noise to the Lord, all the earth!" The Hebrew word used for noise is *rua'*—a battle cry, sound of a trumpet blast, shout in triumph or exaltation. Noise summarizes all these sounds under one label.

Hermann von Helmholtz (1821-1894) stated the best description of noise I found. Helmholtz was a German physicist whose research in physiological acoustics is part of the basis for musical theory, and his research in optical physiology is part of the foundation for visual art theory. Let us look at Helmholtz's description.

> The nature of the difference between musical tones and noises, can generally be determined by attentive aural observation without artificial assistance. We perceive that generally, a noise is accompanied by a rapid alternation of different kinds of sensations of sound. Think, for example, of the rattling of a carriage over granite paving stones, the splashing or seething of a waterfall or of the waves of the sea, rustling of leaves in a wood. In all these cases we have rapid, irregular, but distinctly perceptible alternations of various kinds of sounds, which crop up fitfully. When the wind howls the alternation is slow, the sound slowly and gradually rises and then falls again. It is also more or less possible to separate restlessly alternating sounds [from] the greater number of other noises.... On the other hand, a musical tone strikes the ear as a perfectly undisturbed, uniform sound which remains unattended as long as it exists, and it presents no alternations of various kinds of constituents. To this then corresponds a simple, regular kind of sensations, whereas in a noise many various sensations of musical tone are irregularly mixed up and as it were tumbled together in confusion.[3]

We see noise is random "irregularly mixed, tumbled together in confusion" without cohesion or logic. "Making a joyful noise to the Lord" is for individual or personal use, where we convey to God our heart's intent, which may not make sense to other people, as they do not comprehend our heart. This is the same as singing in the shower or singing when driving alone in the car. In these situations, it does not matter how we sound, whether we are off key, or are singing too loud, are too sharp or flat, because we are singing for personal enjoyment.

When making noise, we make random sounds that accidentally combine; "joyful" gives direction to our sounds. Our use of the phrase "joyful noise" usually means we express a passionate sound in personal worship. God wants us to share with him our heart's worship without barriers, and the way it may come out will only fit together in our heart. This is the intent of personal worship.

To bring works into existence for others, we must make purposeful presentations, as people only see our actions' results, not our heart's intent as God does. We use skill to express our actions so that others grasp our purpose. Psalms 78:72 gives this perspective, "So he [David] shepherded them [the people of Israel] according to the integrity of his heart, and guided them by the *skillfulness* of his hands." Asaph, one of the chief Levites appointed to lead the skilled musicians in ministering to the Lord (1 Chronicles 15 and 16), wrote this psalm. The Hebrew word for "skill" used in this verse is *t'ḇunāh*—meaning: understanding, insight, ability, wisdom. To become skilled in any area takes time. As we develop a skill, we go through a learning process where we learn a medium, make mistakes, find ways to overcome mistakes, search the medium's limits, formulate ideas through the medium, study the ways the medium may express ideas clearly, increase our execution's consistency, along with successfully presenting finished products. When we review the skill acquisition process, recognize we added to our skill, understanding, insights, ability, and wisdom.

Another perspective of skill is in Psalms 33:2-3, "Praise the Lord with the harp, make melody to Him with an instrument of ten strings. Sing to Him a new song; play *skillfully* with a shout of joy." The Hebrew word used is *yāṭaḇ*—meaning: to be good, go well, be glad, to do good, right, to make successful, cause to prosper.

These two Scripture passages give a concise concept of skill.[4] As stated above, skill involves understanding, insight, ability, and wisdom. When we skillfully express a work, it will go well, be pleasing, good, successful, and will prosper. This does not happen when a work's elements are thrown together, illogically, randomly.

Every time, we present a work to other people, we must craft a skilled Expression. If a work is poorly constructed, people will turn away. Expertise takes time to build. It takes practice, working to understand our medium and the way to compose ideas through the medium.

It's like the old joke of a person asking directions in New York City, "How do you get to Carnegie Hall?"

The person answering said, "Practice! Practice! Practice!"

As we work at building our skill level to express ideas proficiently through a medium, we are to practice the correct steps, notes, techniques, etc., or we will not attain our desire. For instance, singing a song for an audience, if we sing the wrong words, we embarrass ourselves through the mistakes, and the audience will not receive the work as we envision.

SYMPHONY ILLUSTRATION

At times, noise is okay, and other times not.
How do we understand the difference?

If you have ever attended a symphony orchestra concert, you already observed the distinction. As you enter the symphony hall and take your seat before the performance, you may notice musicians fine-tuning their instruments. In the string section, the cellist, harpist, and violinist may pluck or strum their instrument's strings to check any last-minute tuning adjustment. In the woodwinds, the bassoons and clarinets are fine-tuning their instruments. In the brass section, the trumpeters blow air through their horns to push any moisture out of the spit valve. Some musicians may practice a section of music they will perform, guaranteeing they command the part. All these sounds are happening at once, along with the sounds of the audience coming in, finding their seats, talking, and projecting their racket all around. We dramatically experience Helmholtz's definition of "noise". At the appointed time, the lights dim, and the audience quiets. The conductor steps onto the stage and the audience may enthusiastically applaud during their walk to the stand. Once the conductor reaches the stand, the audience's applause silences, and the conductor picks up the baton, raising their arms to begin the performance. Then the musicians launch into the score, following the conductor's direction, presenting the music as intended.

The symphony orchestra illustration shows there is a place for noise but also a time to stop the racket and make music. The arts teach us discernment, identifying when random, haphazard sounds are okay, and when to combine elements "purposefully," "logically," and/or "meaningfully". Using the illustration above, let us employ the labels of Noise, and Music or Art to distinguish when noise is okay and when to have a meaningful purpose, where everything comes together, skillfully conveying its maker's intentional ideas and emotions.

ENERGY

Works are a bridge, connecting a maker to an audience.[5] The maker determines how an audience bonds to a work, based on how successful they are at combining elements, along with the level of energy it contains. Good works have more energy than bad works.

What is the energy? Energy may extend from our soul power, and it may proceed from the Holy Spirit. At the end of the third chapter, I identified energy as vitality. The English word, vitality, derives from the Latin, *vitalis*—"pertaining to life". The corresponding word in Greek is *pneuma*—"spirit, life, wind, breath". We recognize when works radiate vital energy or not. Works are waiting for an audience to access their energy. The way we release a work's energy is to engage with a work.

For live performances,[6] performers transmit a work's vigor through the successful execution of their presentation—speaking, acting, dancing, and making music. The audience receives the transmitted energy and replies by broadcasting their positive or negative reactive-energy back to the stage. The performers assimilate the feedback, integrate it, and project their response through the fixed recital-energy projection of the next section to the audience. This give-take-give energy flow will last as long as performers are presenting the work.[7]

Energy may be stored in recorded works. People preserve past performances as recordings of music, drama, and dance. Books, pictures, and other works of art may also contain energy waiting for an audience to release it. To gain access to a work's stored energy, we must listen to music, watch performances, read books, look at artwork, etc. To connect with self-contained or recorded works, we involve ourselves with them more than with live performances. The degree we engage a work determines how we access its energy. If we casually encounter a work, what we receive is minimal. The Bible correlates how we interface with a work as the immature taking in milk and the mature tasting and chewing solid food (Hebrews 5:13-14).

CHRISTIAN SUBJECT MATTER

Many Christian artists like to narrow their emphasis to Christian subjects for a Christian audience. And sometimes makers aim works toward God. We will focus on Christian music in the next few sections and may apply the insights to other areas of art.

Christian subjects are for an exclusively Christian audience, for a variety of purposes. As previously described, a couple questions for makers to consider are "What is the subject's purpose for the audience?" and "What emphasis does the work's experience impart?" These questions help a maker focus a work's Expression, letting them ponder the work through the eyes of its intended audience. It is good also for an audience to be aware of such questions, as it helps show the way artists Express a Content. For people who want to concentrate on making works to a Christian audience, let me encourage you to center attention on *Seeking first the Kingdom of God and His Righteousness…*(Matthew 6:33 KJV). This verse will keep many makers focused as they address topics for a Christian audience having to do with culture, politics, identity, and so on.

WORSHIP

When we offer our works to God as the specific audience, what do we present? This is a loaded question which we will not answer fully or adequately, but we can try to understand its gist. Jesus loved us before we knew Him and gave His life so we may live. When the Holy Spirit gives us a revelation of how much God loves us, we may respond to the revelation and share something with God. What do we give God? Praise, adoration, thanksgiving, obedience, and so much more.

Let us look at a couple of examples of artists who gave God praise and adoration. In January 1547, the Pope appointed Michelangelo (1475-1564) as Chief Architect for St. Peter's Church in Rome, where he redesigned the dome to be aesthetically pleasing and layed out the courtyard. At Michelangelo's request, he did not receive a salary during the time he was architect at St. Peter's, as he saw his service as an act of worship to God.[8] The Holy Spirit inspired and inundated George Frideric Handel (1685-1759) to compose *Messiah's* 260-page manuscript in 24 days, with little sleep or food. When Handel performed the first concert of *Messiah*, the money went to free 142 men from debtor's prison and many, many *Messiah*'s performances provided money to charities—hospitals, feeding the hungry, clothing the naked, fostered orphans.[9] These external acts, apart from the work, also show their maker's heart towards God.

Michelangelo followed inspiration as he designed St. Peter's dome. Inspired vision so seized Handel, he was overwhelmed at rapidly notating the notes of his spiritual encounter while being faithful to the musical experience he envisioned. Audiences listening to *Messiah* may have revelations through the experience. King David's psalms are another example showing how artists gave their heart's expression to God through their works, presenting the works to God as the audience, along with other people that behold the offering.

When we give to God, we may enter a category called worship. Worship[10] is a verb; defined as adoration, homage, and reverent honor given to something or someone, often a deity, but not always. Some synonyms are venerate, reverent-fear, and (in a negative sense) idolize. Worship is an action connected to the heart. All areas of creative-endeavor connect with worship. When we render worship as a noun, it describes the result of the worship-action.

Reflecting on God's love, we may recall his works, his actions toward us, his salvation, his many glories, his intimate holiness, and want to give God adoration, praise, and exaltation. Consider the song, *How Great Thou Art* (1885). When singing this hymn, we proclaim God's works and His salvation, evoking adoration, homage, and reverent-honor which we transmit to God through the heart-connecting action of singing the hymn along with any additional action we may exercise, like raising hands or bowing down.

It is possible to sing songs to God but not connect our heart to the action of singing. This means we are just saying words, not giving worship, as our heart is not in it. God brought this issue up in the Old Testament many times through the prophets to the nation of Israel.

Our contemporary church culture assumes worship is primarily musical. Singing is part of the way we offer adoration to God, but it is *only* part. Worship connects to every area of life, not just one area. What are some ways we express to God our reverence, adoration, and devotion? We may articulate our veneration and prayers through every art medium—dance, music, drama, visual depictions, writing, speaking, and other actions. When we worship, our being inter-connects fully, even may reach the height of our design capacity, as an integrated individual at God's throne, as Moses was in God's presence.

Speaking of Moses, his face glowed for a while, from being in God's presence. I observed this phenomenon twice in my life, with over 15 years separating the incidents. In both instances, while the person worshiped God, their face shone until they stopped.

But most people do not experience this evidence of being in the presence of God. Why not? Maybe some of the answer is in the reply Jesus gave to the Samaritan woman.

But the hour is coming, and is now here, when the true worshipers will worship the Father in spirit and truth, for the Father is seeking such people to worship him. God is spirit, and those who worship him must worship in spirit and truth.

John 4:23-24

Jesus said genuine worship involves spirit and truth. Many times, during the singing part of a church meeting, the songs sung present only feelings (most often sentimentality), without our emotions being grounded in truth. During worship, emotions will arise in response to God's presence without trying to work them up. Let us ask the Holy Spirit to lead us into all the truth (John 16:13). Worshiping God in truth always affects us and our emotions. I believe one of the many reasons God called David a man after God's own heart was that David's worship to God involved his whole being while being grounded in God's Truth.

Another example of worship is the Roman centurion, Cornelius. He is described in Acts 10:2 as "a devout man who feared God with his household, gave alms generously to the people and prayed continually to God". God distinguished Cornelius for his worship by sharing the Holy Spirit with him and his household, which showed salvation included non-Jews. It also demonstrated, Bible teacher and scholar, Derek Prince's (1915-2003) encapsulation of worship: "But few people realize that worship is not primarily an utterance; it is an attitude of the whole being."[11]

CONFUSION

I listened to songs dispatched over Christian radio airwaves and realized the radio hosts and the audience often confused the distinction between Christian subjects and worship. As I paid attention to the songs, I noticed the topics covered: Christian living, songs about God—where praise is passive (as distinct from actively directing praise to God), songs about the presenter's wonderings of life, songs that say God is with me in trouble/He is mighty to save me/God will come through/God is on my side/I can make it, singers preaching to people through their songs, songs of declarations, and occasionally, a song might exclaim God is king, along with a few songs actively giving God praise and adoration.

Confusion occurs because we lump together all these topics as "praise and worship". A vast number of songs on Christian radio do not fit the praise or worship categories. Predominantly, what we hear is entertainment. Entertainment is not bad and is a topic we may pursue, but it should not be mistaken for praise or worship; it is not. To add to the confusion, many churches bring entertainment songs into the singing part of their service, since they presume all songs are the same. Some churches have transitioned away from singing praise songs and worship songs, to sing mostly entertainment songs.

Entertainment is passive. Praise and worship songs are proactive, involving our whole being, where we adore, honor, and venerate God, as God. Praise and worship bring us out from ourselves, moving our focus off ourselves, toward God, on Jesus, as the center of our lives. In this manner, we "turn our eyes upon Jesus and look full in His wonderful face, and the things of this earth will grow strangely dim, in the light of His glory and grace".[12]

Here is the result of genuine praise and worship activity for us: glorifying God alters our perceptions, where our eyes move off ourselves, to realign us to see God as he is. And the outcome of genuine praise and worship for God is that he receives His due reverence since our heart is in it.

IN CONCLUSION

When presenting works to an audience—of other people or to God—let us remember to ask: "What is the subject's purpose for the audience?" and "What emphasis does the work's experience impart?" These questions will help a maker see their works from an audience's perspective. We want the work to be clear, where its aim lands on the intended bull's eye.

Let us understand how an audience grasps our works because this is good communication. Most of the time, works are for other people. As we understand who the work's intended audience is, then we may better understand its context, along with the balance and flow of the work's elements.

---

1. Wilson, Edwin, Goldfarb, Alvin, *Theater: The Lively Art, Fifth Edition*, p. 13 "Although this may not be readily apparent, a necessary element for theater is the audience. In fact, the essence of theater is the interaction between performer and audience. A theater, dance, or musical event is not complete—one could almost say it does not occur—unless there are people to see and hear it. When we read a play in book form, or listen to recorded music, what we experience is similar to looking at a painting or reading a poem; it is a private event, not a public one, and the live performance is re-created and imagined rather than experience first hand."
2. Booth, Eric, *The Everyday Work of Art: how artistic experience can transform your life*, p.140
3. Helmholtz, Hermann, *On the Sensation of Tone*, p.7-8
4. Additionally, the Hebrew word *hāk'māh* meaning wisdom, skill, and learning, is used in Exodus 36:1-2, "Bezalel and Oholiab and every craftsman in whom the Lord has put his *skill* and intelligence to know how to do any work in the construction of the sanctuary shall work in accordance with all the Lord

commanded. And Moses called Bezalel and Oholiab and every craftsman in whose mind the Lord had put *skill*, everyone whose heart stirred him to come and do the work."

5. Dewey, John, *Art As Experience*, p. 106 "The work of art is complete only as it works in the experience of others than the one who created it. Thus language involves what logicians call a triadic relation. There is the speaker, the thing said, and the one spoken to. The external object, the product of art, is the connecting link between artist and audience."

 Seashore, Carl, *Psychology of Music*, p.13-14, 23-26 Seashore gives a connecting link of "musician", "music" and "listener".

6. A good description of the difference between works presented live and self-contained works, is to compare film and live theater, described in Edwin Wilson and Alvin Goldfarb's book, *Theater: The Lively Art, Fifth Edition*, p. 9. "The most significant difference between films and theater is the *relationship between the performer and the audience*. The experience of being in the presence of the performer is more important to theater than anything else. No matter how closely a film follows the story of a play, no matter how involved we are with the people on the screen, we are always in the presence of an *image*, never a person."

 My summation of this point: a film is an *image* of the story, and the audience is in the *presence* of an *image*; in live theater we are in the *presence* of a story, along with the actors being in the *presence* of the audience.

7. ibid, p. 9 "At the heart of the theater experience, therefore, is the performer-audience relationship—the immediate, personal exchange whose chemistry and magic give theater its special quality. During a Stage performance the actresses and actors can hear laughter, can sense silence, and can feel tension in the audience. In short, the audience can affect, and in subtle ways change, the performance."

8. Vasari, *Lives of the Artists*, p. 387 "Then Michelangelo, seeing the great trust and confidence that the Pope reposed in him, wanted to demonstrate his own good will by having it declared in the papal decree that he was devoting his time to the fabric for the love of God, and without any other reward." Then from *Lives of the Artists* footnote: "Michelangelo's appointment as Chief Architect to St. Peter's was confirmed in January 1547. He remained responsible for this tremendous undertaking until his death."

9. Kavanaugh, Patrick, *The Spiritual Lives of Great Composers*, Chapter One - George Fredric Handel, p. 3-9

10. Scripture uses several words for "worship". The Hebrew word, *šāḥāh*, means: to bow down, to weigh down, cause to bow; the Hebrew word *s'gid*, means to worship, pay honor; the Greek word, *proskyneō*, means: to do reverence or homage by kissing the hand, used in New Testament to do reverence or honor by prostration, to pay divine homage, worship, adore, to bow one's self in adoration, fall down before; the Greek word, *latreuō*, means: to be a servant, to serve, to render religious service and homage, worship, to offer sacrifices, present offerings, serve, worship; the Greek word, *latreia*, means: service, servitude, religious service, worship; the Greek word, *eusebeō*, means: to exercise piety, when directed towards a deity, to worship; and when directed towards

relatives, to be dutiful; the Greek word, *sebō*, means: to stand in awe, to venerate, reverence, worship, adore.

11. I heard Derek Prince say this several times. As I looked up where he wrote this, it is found in his book, *Thanksgiving, Praise and Worship* (1991), page 47.

12. Helen Howarth Lemmel (1863-1961), *Turn Your Eyes upon Jesus* ©1922

6

SIGNIFICANT FORM

In the Introduction, I shared how I grew up in church and, as someone interested in art, wanted to learn the biblical view of art. I read Francis Schaeffer, H.R. Rookmaaker, and Frank(y) Schaeffer's available writings. Their writings encouraged me, revealing how the Bible gives a positive portrayal of art. I considered the creative works Christians made at the time; I meditated on the use of music, my knowledge of contemporary painters, and the increasing acceptance of drama and dance in churches. Reflecting on these observations, I asked God, "With all these developments, why are Christians not affecting the arts and culture?" God answered my query 20 years later.

I did not realize I had to learn many things before I could understand God's answer. For me to be faithful with God's reply, I had to go through art school and digest the concepts taught, engage other cultures with some international travel, expand my creating knowledge, gain teaching experience, and cultivate an increased awareness of people's creative endeavors, Christian and non-Christian.

SIGNIFICANT FORM

The answer came as I read a book I bought at a thrift store, written in 1914 by Clive Bell (1881-1964) entitled *Art*. Clive Bell was a critic connected with the Bloomsbury Group in England. I surveyed his life and doubt he was a Christian. But Bell wrote a sentence in his book which sparked a new point of view in me: "Don't waste your time and energy on things that don't matter: concentrate on what does: concentrate on the creation of significant form."[1]

My view of "significant form" is not necessarily the same as Clive Bell's. I will not compare his meaning to mine, because it does not matter. The Holy Spirit illuminated the "significant form" concept as the answer to my prayer when I was ready to comprehend it. Bell's sentence triggered many thoughts in my head. I recalled my prayer-question of why Christians do not affect culture. In my mind, an image-train whirled through art history, highlighting various works and the way they influenced their time. Then I considered works made today. These images flashed through my mind, converging through the phrase "significant form". Let me now make some sense of the insight flashes that shaped and formed into a developed thought.

From its very beginning, Art has been used to express ideas. For now, we will narrow our focus to the visual arts; though, as I stated before, the insights apply to all the arts. Once churches used art, its purpose was to display the stories and ideas of the Bible for illiterate congregations. Through the centuries, artists sought to better convey biblical ideas, leading the congregation to a deeper understanding of God. Art history of the Late Middle Ages and Renaissance shows the way artists searched to express the profound meanings of Scriptures. New styles and innovations occurred as artists sought to articulate deep Scriptural truth for their time.

For example, images we are familiar with from the Renaissance are Leonardo da Vinci's *Last Supper*, Michelangelo's murals in the Sistine Chapel—on the ceiling the stories in Genesis and on the end wall the *Last Judgment*, Albrecht Durer's wood-cut print *Four Horsemen of the Apocalypse*, Durer's drawing study of hands in a praying position for a painting of St. Peter, which we know as *The Praying Hands*. Understandably, the works of great artists often have lasting influence.

FORMS CHANGE

Bell asked a question in his book, "But how comes it that the art of one age differs from that of another? At first sight it seems odd that art, which is the expression of man's sense of significance of form, should vary even superficially from age to age."[2]

Have you wondered how society and culture change? How is it that what was fashionable in 14th century China, 15th century Italy, 16th century Flanders, and 18th century France were not the same and differ still from today's fashion? Technology influences and shapes each time-period. Events of history affect societal reasoning in both positive and negative ways.

As an example, let us review technological development for listening to music. Songs recorded on discs, circa 1901, replaced the wax cylinder recordings used for the Cylinder Phonograph and Cylinder Gramophone. Initially, the record disc was rubber, then changed to shellac discs, before vinyl became the standard which played on a phonograph, first at 78 rotations per minute (rpm), replaced by 45 rpm and 33 rpm. Magnetic tape, and the smaller cassette tapes was used to record and playback sound until the digital recording format became the norm. Digital formatting has shaped our current listening approach to music: songs were first put on compact discs (CD's), then stored and retrieved on a computer's hard drive as a sound file (mp3's), and later the sound file streamed over the internet which our computer devices access so we may listen to the recording through the computer/digital audio speakers or head/earphones.[3]

In this brief survey of the progression of music technology, we notice the way each advance shaped personal music enjoyment, along with the hidden assumptions and expectations influencing the way we perceive and approach music. Let us also consider the way we use social media; in the way we share works and espouse content. The expanding manner through which we experience works shows that changes in style come as a natural development.

CHRISTIAN FORMS TODAY

While reflecting upon art history through the important works, I asked myself why these works were significant for their time periods and what significant forms the artists used to bring out the truths they sought. Then I turned my attention to the present and asked, "What significant forms are Christians and churches using today?"

We can peek in a Christian bookstore for an answer to the last question. We will see mass-produced reproductions of the Renaissance images, *Praying Hands* or the *Last Supper*. We can find images of Jesus from the late 1800s, and Sunday school style illustrations. We find Thomas Kinkade's (1958-2012) cottage pictures, some sugary beach photographs or nature scenes, and knick-knacks with Scripture on them. A lot of what we observe in books, music, and assorted ornaments is only for Christian entertainment. We could deposit two thirds of the stuff in Christian bookstores in a trash bin and not miss it because most products target the sentimental emotions of its audience.[4]

Today, the art images most familiar to us are around 125-500 years old; these representations are rehashed and reused, over and over and over and over again. If a Christian bookstore reflects our taste and beliefs, does the display mean our beliefs are petrified, shallow, without life? Our faith is deeper than the shallowness of a store, but is this the perception we project?

SENSITIVITY TO SIGNIFICANT FORM

God answered my prayer when I was ready to understand.
God's answer: concentrate on the creation of significant form.

What is the meaning of significant? Let us combine dictionaries to come up with a comprehensive definition. Significance is a noun, described as: 1) the quality or state of being significant, state of importance; 2) having meaning, import, consequence; 3) signified through word or expression; 4) a meaning implied or expressed; 5) statistical significance. The word significant comes from the Latin *significantia*—which is: "meaning, force, energy"; the root word being *significns*—to signify.

Significant form is a form that relevantly conveys the energized force of an idea, touching at levels deeper than clichés do. We can even say that significant form expresses the mystery, meaning, consequence, and life of God's Love and Truth for a culture or time-period, at least until we need to use a fresh approach. Relevant forms express Scriptural truth to every area God's Kingdom touches. Works we recognize as significant not only convey truth but have vital power to draw an audience. When a form significantly conveys its idea, we respond to its obviousness.

For instance, how might an artist give form to the Bible verse below, through his or her preferred medium.

"Am I a God near at hand" says the Lord, "And not a God afar off? Can anyone hide himself in secret places, so I shall not see him?" says the Lord. "Do I not fill heaven and earth?" says the Lord.

Jeremiah 23: 23-24, NKJV[5]

I understand I present this verse out of its context, and there are several verses which state that God is near,[6] but this statement shows how God is *also* "afar off," portraying God in a larger perspective. Here we realize God as God, then grasp the reality that he fills the heavens and the earth. God is so much more than we conceive, and we may receive revelational glimpses of his character as the Holy Spirit leads us into his Holiness; as Saint Paul experienced on his way to Damascus (Acts 9:1-19), and as Saint John received revelation on Patmos (Revelation 1). The way we give form to Jeremiah 23:23 is important, because the form determines if we express the verse truthfully. I will not relay my ideas on a relevant form for the verse, so you may be free with your thoughts. As you consider the verse and explore its context, go past the clichés because God is so much more than trite platitudes. Even ask God for revelation.

The Church quit looking for significant forms expressing the cross and resurrection for this age. In other words, it kept its salt to itself and kept its light inside the doors of its box. By remaining in a sacred/secular mindset, society and culture are locked in status quo, and our responses react to and condemn society's happenings. Reacting *always* follows; ask any ballroom dancer. Therefore, if we are to influence our culture, we must lead the dance. Let us learn to have a "sensibility to the profound significance of form and the power of creation".[7] When we do, we imitate our Creator.

FATHER COUTURIER'S INFLUENCE

French Dominican priests, Father M. A. Couturier (1897-1954),[8] and Father Pie-Raymond Régamey (1900-1996), were for a time the chief editors of a French Ecclesiastical magazine, *L'Art Sacré*, which sought to educate its readers on significant form. These Catholic priests advocated a re-introduction of living art back into the Church. They saw the Catholic Church rehashing old clichés, not digging into forms effectively significant for their present culture. Father Couturier's revolutionary approach was to use many non-Christian artists of the time, "wildflowers" he called them, to make and decorate churches,[9] because he did not see many high caliber "cultivated flowers"—Christian artists. The wildflower artists, along with a few cultivated flowers, decorated churches in France, with paintings, sculptures, tapestries, stained glass, ceramics, and mosaics. The churches Father Couturier influenced: Chapelle du Rosaire de Venice (Chapel of the Rosary of Venice, France), also called The Venice Chapel and/or Matisse's Chapel, decorated by artist Henri Matisse;[10] Chapelle Notre Dame du Haut de Ronchamp (The Chapel of our Lady of the Heights in Ronchamp),[11] designed by architect Le Corbusier; Eglise du Notre-Dame de Toute Grâce du Plateau d'Assy (Church of Our Lady Full of Grace of the Assy Plateau),[12] works in the church by Pierre Bonnard, Fernand Léger, Jean Lurçat, Paul Cosandier, Germaine Richier, Georges Rouault, Jean Bazaine, Henri Matisse, Georges Braque, Jacques Lipchitz, Marc Chagall, Constant Demaison, Ladislas Kijno, Claude Mary, Carlo Sergio Signori, and Théodore Strawinsky; and finally Eglise du Sacré Coeur d'Audincourt (Church of the Sacred Heart of Audincourt),[13] with works in the church by Fernand Léger, Jean Bazaine, and Jean Le Meal. Father Couturier even thought he could persuade Picasso to decorate a church, but died before talking to him.[14]

King David brought skilled musicians together in ancient Israel when he established systematic worship before God. Similarly, Father Couturier and other like-minded priests sought to bring to God the best artists available. For some of these artists, the works they made in these churches are distinguished as among their best. The French government recognized the endeavors, classifying the church at Assy as a French historic monument, and the chapel at Haut as a cultural landmark. UNESCO acknowledged the chapel at Ronchamp as a World Heritage site.

SOULISH

Father Couturier observed most works we promote as spiritual works in Western Christendom are rather soulish—products re-enforcing our human soul-nature and its manner. This is an issue he tried to address with *L'Art Sacré*, and by influencing the artists commissioned to make works in the French churches listed above. In today's time, we often confuse soulish works as spiritual.

Let us define "soulish": it is where the self is the center[15] even if God is talked about. Let us look at some background to understand our "soulish" preferences. Our personhood has three basic areas: body, soul, and spirit.[16] The body is our material, physical self, housing our senses which interact with the physical world and other people. With the rise of psychology—the study of the soul—we have a better understanding of how the soul operates. Our soul comprises personality, character, emotions, intellect (ways of thinking), and will (our decisions, drive, and subsequent actions). Our spirit energizes our being—consciousness is synonymous with our spirit; and our conscious connects to our spirit. Each area has both positive and negative approaches.[17]

The Greek word for soul is *psuche*, the transliteration of which is "psyche". *Psuche's* adjective form, *psuchikos,* describes an action initiated by the soul. Linguistic and Biblical scholars agree the clearest English translation of *psuchikos* is soulish.[18]

Since the Fall of Adam, our soul has directed our personhood. When God reconciled us to himself through Jesus' death and resurrection, our spirit was enlivened; God communicates with us, Spirit to spirit. When we have a war inside our-self, often our soul is asserting its control over us.[19]

This makes me wonder, "Can we distinguish between soul and spirit?" On the surface, it does not seem we can. To reinforce a soulish orientation, the adversary sets up societal systems geared to some aspect of the soul. These systems teach us to conform to expectations, thus shaping our tastes to prefer shallow, mediocre experiences. Mediocrity reinforces the accuser's lie that we are not creative. We brought soul-centered philosophy into churches, often influencing us more than spirit to Spirit communication with God. Christian works today seem to reinforce a soulish-self, instead of pointing at *transforming* to righteousness. Many church systems buttress a cheap sacred/secular soul-centeredness. The enemy has worked hard to shift our focus to the inconsequential, where we do not pursue excellence or significance but conformity to soul-centered views and behaviors. Cultural conditioning, along with our churchy programming, mold us to prefer things appealing to our emotions and self-centeredness. Soulishness permeates our lives more than we realize often driving us to embrace superficiality in life activities and products.

We, as the Bride of Christ, are marrying a Groom who is excellent, expressing eternal significance. If we are to be like Christ, then we also are to pursue significance beyond our soul, even as it touches the Eternal. Do our actions and works give the impression we seek such weighty considerations? Often, no. Maybe one reason is, we do not ask the significant questions. Why should we ask the hard life questions when we assume the questions are secular? We *do* have answers to life's questions, which begin in Jesus. But I challenge our assumptions over the manner we apply biblical solutions to our lives—and how we enforce the same on others.

Do our assumptions reflect Jesus' agape? We assume we must *compel* an outward moral conformity, but this drives people from Jesus, for there is no love to it. By observing the Scribes and Pharisees' many interactions with Jesus, as we pursue moral rightness above Agape, we remain soulish. When our focus centers on our soul, we do not seek beyond it, where Significance roams. Significance is an elusive beast that does not readily embrace anyone, only those who know how to feed it. Most people do not feed true significance. Comfortable mediocrity is what we display through the abundance of cliched works people make and consume. I am not criticizing a maker's motive for making works, even to God. I assume good intentions. But keep in mind, sincerity does not guarantee the right outcome. We test the work itself, and its effect, asking, "Does it succeed in the desired impact its maker had in mind?"

A SONG EXAMPLE

With this in mind, let us consider a couple of examples from Christian culture. First, we will look at a song example then after, a picture example. Remember, I am not criticizing a maker's motive for making works. I assume good intentions.

We will begin with the song example still sung in many churches, *Open the Eyes of My Heart,* written by Paul Baloche © 1997, published through Integrity's Hosanna! Music (ASCAP) (adm at IntegratedRights.com). Since this song is more than twenty years old, we can look at it without emotion overshadowing us.

This song is based on Ephesians 1:17-25 and the author's inspiration from reading it. The author's desire, and our desire as we sing, that we perceive God afresh, is a good desire to express.

The reason I offer this song as an example is because of a couple words that distract from the song's intention. For some who sing this song, the lyrics give the impression that God isn't already exalted with his train filling the temple (Isaiah 6:1). In this song, where is God at? I would say he is perceived at our level. (If you must justify a maker's intent, saying, "they meant ___," then they failed to express their idea clearly.) I suggest this song would have a greater impact and be theologically sound, with a minor change: taking out the word "To" and replace it with "For You are". This minor change clarifies the author's intent, aligning to its Scriptural bases. I see this bus a positive example of testing works.

When we examine and test works, we not only look at the weight placement of an Idea and its Expression, we also ask, "Did the author succeed at clearly articulating their work?" All audiences should ask this question toward every work, even of this book. The basic answer is "yes," "no," and "sort of".

Once we exalt God, raising our viewpoint beyond our soul, to an eternal perspective, as The Revelation of St. John, Chapter One presents, we are changed. I believe this is what Paul Baloche wanted to articulate in his song.

Often the correct image, phase, perspective does not produce itself immediately during the creative process. It takes a hard examination to bring a work to the place it is able to hold up to every test of its audience, every time it is experienced. As the work is refined outside the individual, the Eternal perspective can present itself.

Take a look at songs used in your church. The songs that position God at the human level do not guide the congregation to let go of their soulishness and enter true worship to God. The songs we typically sing are geared to only stir our emotions: i.e., God loves me, I am forgiven, I am not alone, God fill me, God help me, I want God more, etc. Everyone experiences times when we express such sentiments. However, when the focus *stays* centered on the self, our image of Jesus becomes distorted because *we* have become the center. We can examine the types of songs sung in churches and test their weight by asking if a song has more of a "me" or "I" focus, even if God is mentioned. The songs centered on self, place a weightier emphasis on emotions than on who God is. They caress the soul without bringing us into God's presence, though our stirred-up soul makes us feel we are.

Beyond individual songs, there is a trend I observed in churches during the music and song time. I am making a generalization by combining various church traditions (styles) in which the musical portion of a service is structured to last an hour. A team of musicians seeks to work up the congregation's emotion by singing a song for 10-20 minutes. In an hour, we sing 4 to 6 songs. I am not opposed to singing a song for a while, but when it happens, it meets a specific purpose or as a response to the Holy Spirit. This occurrence may happen infrequently or even frequently, but not in each service nor with every song. We are not to manipulate a congregation into an emotional state; this tactic is not apart of God's Agape. Manipulating emotions strokes the ego, placing emotion ahead of God. When emotion leads, the works that follow are usually soulish.

KING DAVID'S PATTERN

In contrast, let us contemplate King David's probable view of worship. Psalm 100 gives a clue. David used the tabernacle as a pattern. Verse 4 says, "Enter his gates with thanksgiving and his courts with praise." The Hebrew word for *thanksgiving* is *to̱dāh*, meaning thank-offering, confession of thankfulness, song of thankfulness. Thanksgiving is the speaking of the excellence of a person or object, with a focus on the personal gratitude of the speaker. The Hebrew word for *praise* is *t'hillāh,* meaning praise, renown, glory. Praise is proclaiming the excellence, prominence, glory of a person or object. Thanksgiving and Praise are two categories that David wrote for. He wrote for another song category called "Songs of Ascent," which people sang to prepare themselves as they walked up to the tabernacle before they entered the gates with thanksgiving. Should we put *Open the Eyes of My Heart*, in the category of Songs of Ascent, Thanksgiving, or Praise? The answer is Songs of Ascent.

With the tabernacle model, "entering the gates with thanksgiving" focuses on God's goodness, which is the reason for offering thanksgiving. The songs of praise are different at the outer courts than the inner courts. Not far past the gate, as we enter the outer court, the praises reflect how God brought us out of darkness, saved us, brought us to life and into a relationship with himself. Between the inner and outer courts are located the symbols of God's redemption: the altar of sacrifice, which corresponds to the cross, and the washbasin correlates to the blood of Christ. Then, moving to the inner courts, our attention turns away from ourselves and towards God, to His deeds, His greatness, and His glory.[20]

After the courts of praise, the next major category is worship in the Holy Place. In the Old Testament, priests had to meet special requirements before entering the Holy Place. Jesus, as the high priest and the sacrifice, satisfied every requirement to bring us into God's presence. Language is different in the Holy Place from the courts of praise; personal pronouns are not commonly used, as the Holy Place is not about us. In the Holy Place, the central characteristic of God's nature we worshipfully expound is his Holiness; we may also assert God's loving-kindness, and be silent to hear God's voice.

The Tabernacle/Temple pattern is not the only template. We may explore a pattern where we come to the King's Throne. The Holy Spirit may illuminate other models as well. The goal for a pattern is to convey us into a deeper Presence of God. Patterns connect with significance more than surface styles of worship do. Styles embody various genres which may move through a praise and worship template. Styles are not patterns or models.[21]

Overall, three quarters or more of the contemporary songs sung in churches are Songs of Ascent, and maybe Songs of Praise that are only proper just past the gates, not for the inner courts. Most churches today present a music experience that does not touch significance, which means most of the time we are not entering God's presence. Many songs we sing in church make our soul feel good with sentiment, so we assume we are before God's presence, though in reality, we are outside the Gates.[22] But we can draw near to God. Therefore, let us go through the gates with thanksgiving, to enter the courts of praise, extolling God's greatness, and loving-kindness, proceeding to enter the Holy Place of God's Holy Presence.

A PICTURE EXAMPLE

Before giving an example, let me provide some background. There is a phenomenon touching visual art, called kitsch. According to *The Oxford Dictionary of Art,* kitsch is the "German term for vulgar trash. Its application ranged from commercial atrocities such as tourist souvenirs to any pretended art, which is considered lacking in honesty or vigor."[23] This definition shows the range kitsch has but does not help us to understand what it is. So, let us combine several other dictionaries to define kitsch, as something tawdry, vulgar, pretentious that appeals to sentimental, popular, undiscriminating taste. Some synonyms are bad taste, vulgar, course, tasteless, garish. The primary use we are discussing are works with content that lacks honesty or vigor, targeting an audience's sentimentality.

In 1939, art critic Clement Greenberg (1909-1994) brought kitsch to the American public's attention in his article, *Avant-Garde and Kitsch.* The second half of his article is still the best summation and overview of the kitsch phenomenon. I will not explain all Greenberg expounded on, but I will simplify what kitsch amounts to.

Kitsch places sentimental emotion first, as a work's most important aspect, which sets the subject into a minor role. In contrast, art may produce emotion as a response to the subject, but the subject is first and emotion second. Kitsch emphasizes superficial formulas and clichés to induce sentimentality, so the consumer does not waste energy on thinking. Kitsch's character is revealed through clichés. Greenberg stated that kitsch is now the universal cultural product. From my travels around the world, I observed this to be true.

The nature of kitsch is to render the *what-of-the-subject* as more important than *how-the-subject-is-expressed.*[24] Kitsch's subject matter (its *what*) is sentimental emotion which permeates the work, be that subject a child, historic person, animal, building, place, or some other object. You may have seen an illustration of a child in a thrift store. Let us use the child picture as an example. Imagine the subject is a girl in a pink dress, sitting in a chair with toys on the floor. We like a picture of a child because the she is cute. It does not matter whether the girl's hair is long, shoulder-length, or short; we will feel the same no matter which element used. If we change the dress' color to yellow, our sentiment will not alter. Nor would our feelings change whether the girl is in another room or an outdoor setting. If we switch the girl out for a boy, our emotions will stay the same as long as the child is cute. We only care about the emotion the cute child picture stirs up, not the picture itself.[25]

Adjustments to a "good" work of art might ruin the picture, and alterations to a "bad" work may improve it. With kitsch, changes do not matter, provided its sentimental emotion is apparent. Kitsch does not seek for truth but proclaims clichés, reinforcing a shallow view of life. For this reason, kitsch is not classified as "art," it is an "anti-art". If you look at a work while imagining an alteration to its subject, and the modification does not disturb its overall impact (gestalt), you are not looking at "art" but a kitsch decoration. Art, in contrast, may evoke emotion in response to the subject, but here the subject is central and the emotion secondary. Art may go deeper than surface sentiment even to express some truth, the way Jesus' parables do, or hymns in the hymnal.

Let me call to mind a picture most American Christians have seen, one of Thomas Kinkade's (1958-2012) cottage paintings. A specific picture does not matter, because they are all similar. The subject of Kinkade's pictures is sentimental emotion that arises in his audience. If we swap the forest cottage for an 1890s Victorian house, or a 1920s prairie style home, or a 1950s modern style house, the changes will not matter as long as our sentiment is stirred, nor does switching the background from woods to a seacoast or a town street. Our feelings about the picture will remain the same because the picture's subject is sentimentality and not the specific house in its setting.

In a Christian bookstore, most-to-all of its pictures and knick-knacks arouse sentimentality in the audience; we do not respond to the image itself, as itself. Father Couturier made a similar observation in 1950:

> Make no mistake about it: the popularity of the sentimental 'devotional' art is due not to the abilities of the hard-sell merchants, but to the fact that the Christian people, with the clergy in the lead, unconsciously recognize themselves in it and are pleased with what they see.[26]

The subject of kitsch varies, but sentimental emotion is kitsch's meaning. Kitsch, like morality, is easy to understand. "Typical consumers of kitsch are pleased not only because they respond spontaneously, but also because they know they are responding in the right kind of way."[27] Because Art expresses something beyond sugary sentiment, in order to understand what the "something" is, we may need to exert energy to grasp a work's meaning, as Jesus' audiences indeed had to do. With kitsch, we keep our energy to ourselves, because trite clichés require nothing from us. Kitsch does not reveal truth, but rather our preference for soulish sugar rushes.

COMMENTS ON THE REST OF THE ARTS

Here in the present, when we survey the works Christians make, do they convey significance to an audience? It is the rare exception that does. Mel Gibson's *The Passion of the Christ* (2004) is one example of a rare exception. Most Christians only want to get a message across, but have not considered choreographer Agnes de Mille's (1905-1993) wisdom on this topic: "Great messages are voiced greatly. This is the basis and validity of the art experience."[28] We cannot communicate significant messages through clichés' shallowness.

Truth is outside of our-self and our stirred-up emotions.

Truth is not wimpy, but powerful and life-filling. Artists try to present Truth's substance through their mediums, sometimes with success. But often, Christians confuse the distinction between stirred-up emotions and significant form. Therefore, Christian Art's influence on culture is marginal.

BEAUTY

Only now as we contemplate significance, are we ready to look at beauty. The books on philosophy and aesthetics that deal with beauty can be confusing. Beauty has an eternal aspect, which is the reason we have trouble defining its nature. We assume beauty is a surface issue. We use words like attractive, good-looking, lovely, pleasing, handsome, pretty, as synonymous with beauty; these words reinforce our superficial viewpoint. But beauty's depth is profound.

Plotinus (204-269 AD) wrote in *The Enneads*:

> This, then, is how the material thing becomes beautiful—by communicating in the thought that flows from the Divine.[29]

Plotinus was not a Christian, but I think he understood that beauty is not really in the eye of the beholder. Plotinus recognized that a divine "flow" may infuse a work. When a work has a "flow from the Divine," it goes beyond a surface presentation to a deepness that possesses a quality of being filled with strength and power, we describe as "beautiful" even when the work is not attractive. Beauty's depth transmits Truth. Beauty and Truth are intimately connected, and if Truth is not expressed, the work is shallow. Surface works can be pleasing, but, either conceptually, aesthetically, and/or spiritually, lack depth's vigor.

Our desire for beauty is natural, being part of the make-up of God's image. I see beauty as an aspect of God's love. As we seek to present the Holy Spirit's inspiration clearly, God's Spirit may satiate the work with his life. Beauty may be a by-product to significance, displaying God's character and glory. And God enjoys sharing beauty with us and through us.

Pope John Paul II communicates the Christian take on beauty. I will quote a couple of passages and I recommend reading the *Letter of His Holiness Pope John Paul II to Artists* (1999) for yourself.

> On the threshold of the Third Millennium, my hope for all of you who are artists is that you will have an especially intense experience of creative inspiration. May the beauty which you pass on to generations still to come be such that it will stir them to wonder! Faced with the sacredness of life and of the human person, and before the marvels of the universe, wonder is the only appropriate attitude.[30]

> Beauty is a key to the mystery and a call to transcendence. It is an invitation to savor life and to dream of the future. That is why the beauty of created things can never fully satisfy. It stirs that hidden nostalgia for God which a lover of beauty like Saint Augustine could express in incomparable terms: 'Late have I loved you, beauty so old and so new: late have I loved you!'.

> Artists of the world, may your many different paths all lead to that infinite Ocean of beauty where wonder becomes awe, exhilaration, unspeakable joy.

> May you be guided and inspired by the mystery of the Risen Christ, whom the Church in these days contemplates with joy.[31]

COMMUNICATING SIGNIFICANCE

We rarely analyze how we express the Holy Spirit's inspirations. The images and ideas God gives us, we translate, condense, then present through our chosen medium. The way we do this becomes crucial. Each artistic discipline processes images inspired by the Holy Spirit, but the artistic medium influences how an image is used.

Over the years, I talked with a few people making "prophetic art".[32] After seeing their works, I asked each person why they placed images in the picture-location they did? Everyone replied the same, saying, "It is what God showed me." I believe God showed these artists various images, while impressing a meaning to them. Visual impressions can come as a singular picture, but commonly are transmitted through sequenced images, like a movie, in which moving pictures and words may appear, and/or a whole concept, along with its various nuances, will imprint over an iconic representation. It is challenging to know how to distill this array to a single point picture that communicates the whole meaning. People combine the images they have in their heads, sometimes logically and other times less so.

Often, "prophetic" artists do not ask the Holy Spirit questions about the images they receive. Maybe they do not know that in every art form placement is part of meaning. For instance, God shows a person an image of a window. A window has a generalized symbolic meaning of seeing through to somewhere else. I would ask what type of window: a farmhouse window, commercial building window, a Gothic window, or a window from a burned-out building; each window-type gives a specific metaphor to the image. The picture's specific style can affect its meaning. Compositional location also influences meaning: where we place the window on a page; in the center, upper left corner, lower right, etc., each location can communicate meaning along with the balance and flow for the overall aim of the picture. When we interact with the Holy Spirit about the representations, he will clarify his intention with the image. Therefore, ask God how and where to use each image. He will refine and shed light on how to use the impressions, in a manner that brings out the meaning's fullness, so God's life touches people. Many Christian individuals working within a framework labeled "prophetic art" stay at the surface; visions are just put down, which does not differ from a New Age-Spiritual/Visionary art approach.

The Holy Spirit gives images that tell-forth and that fore-tell. Therefore, we must be more active in how we receive images by asking God questions on the way to use each image, in placement and style. We may also need to ask God to fill us with his ability to carry out the imagery shown to us, so we will not distort his intention towards the representations. Let us bear in mind that prophetic art must succeed as both prophecy *and* art, or it will not last beyond the moment.

Another important aspect of how we communicate the impressions God gives, pertains to situations where we are to share an inspired image or word in the presence of a congregation. When we disclose the revelation, do we dilute the Holy Spirit's intention by adding to the revealed image our views and opinions? Additionally, we are to discern how the images the Holy Spirit gives us interrelate with the images he gives to others.

The Apostle Paul wrote about this:

> *What then brothers? When you come together, each one has a hymn, a teaching, a revelation, a tongue, or an interpretation. Let all things be done for building up.*
>
> 1 Corinthians 14:26

This verse shows that we have one piece of a puzzle, and we are to present our Holy Spirit inspired image alongside the offerings of others, into a complete and integrated image. As with any picture puzzle, our piece installs in only one spot. When we force a fit, we misrepresent the Holy Spirit's impression with an incomplete and/or incorrect perspective.

We often spout out what God reveals without asking him about when and how to share it. Our egocentric impulses with God's revelation become like flinging paint onto a wall: random, irregularly mixed, tumbled together without cohesiveness—noise. Over the years, I have experienced some church meetings where an individual speaks a "prophetic word" to their congregation. Sometimes the word fits into the unified-complete image of the service, but at other times, the word moves the congregation away from the Holy Spirit's observed intention. We can learn discernment, as we present our piece of revelation into a shared gathering. Love does not contain confusing noise, as 1 Corinthians 13 articulates.

CULTURAL RELEVANCE

We have a natural human desire to connect to our culture; more than just connecting, we want to wield a positive influence. Christians have debated through the centuries various ways to affect culture. The issues boil down to influence or domination.

The primary way we interact with culture is through Jesus' love. Missionaries have sought to communicate God's love to many unreached people groups, and they looked for examples already existing in those cultures that communicate God's love in a manner the society would understand. The label used at the end of the 20th century for this approach was "culturally relevant examples," such as "the peace child" in Indonesia;[33] and the way the Ancient Chinese language base-characters, which pre-date the Bible, convey the fundamental concepts of Genesis.[34]

The present meaning of cultural relevance in world missions seems to have been redefined as conforming to a society's culture. I do not advocate we make "culturally relevant" works of art. I believe we should *impact* or *inspire* culture, not *follow*. Our idea of impact *still* seems to emphasize either influence or domination. Each view shapes how we relate to people and to God, thereby affecting the manner we express the Holy Spirit's inspirations. Over the last 2000 years, Christians employed both methods at different times and different settings. I encourage you to consider for yourself how influence versus domination forms the Church's cultural worldview. Which in turn shapes the way our works influence others.

Let us end this chapter reflecting on the question, "Do our works convey significance?" Jesus, as the Way, the Truth, and Life (John 14:6), is significant. When we trivialize Jesus through sentimental emotion or a cliché, God's Kingdom has little impact on people or the surrounding culture. For this reason, we ask the Holy Spirit's guidance for the effectual manner that conveys his substance and consequence.

---

1. Bell, Clive, *Art,* p. 41
2. Bell, Clive, *Art,* p. 145
3. Summerized from https://en.wikipedia.org/wiki/Phonograph
4. Erik Routley, in his book *The Church and Music,* defined sentimentality on p. 179, ". . . sentimentality is emotional content backed by no solid truth, a show of feeling with no intention of consequent honesty . . .." This is the clearest definition for sentimentality I found.
5. This verse was presented by John Cameron, in the context of Jeremiah 23:21-24, at the 2019 Arise Conference, New Zealand, which I viewed on Daystar Television Network, July 2019. https://www.ariseconference.org.nz.
6. Deuteronomy 4:7, Deuteronomy 31:6, Zephaniah 3:17, Matthew 28:20
7. Bell, Clive, *Art,* p. 127
8. Summerized from https://en.wikipedia.org/wiki/Marie-Alain_Couturier
9. Couturier, M. –A., *Sacred Art,* p. 144-145
10. https://en.wikipedia.org/wiki/Chapelle_du_Rosaire_de_Vence
11. https://en.wikipedia.org/wiki/Notre_Dame_du_Haut_de_Ronchamp
12. https://en.wikipedia.org/wiki/%C3%89glise_Notre-Dame_de_Toute_Gr%C3%A2ce_du_Plateau_d%27Assy
13. http://www.artway.eu/content.php?id=796&lang=en&action=show
14. Couturier, M. –A., *Sacred Art,* p. 158
15. Nee, Watchman, *The Spiritual Man* (in Three Volumes), Vol. 1, Part 3 The Soul, Chapter 2—The Experience of Soulish Believers, p.158. Watchman Nee clarified what "the self is the center" means: "Christians who thrive on the soul life are very proud. This is because they make the self the center. However much they may try to give the glory to God and acknowledge any merit as of God's grace, carnal believers have their mind set on the self."
16. 1 Thessalonians 5:23
17. Human nature is part of body and soul. Each person's soul operates independently. Our soul uses free will in its decision making, which separates us from a hive mentality.

18. *Psuchikos* has been translated into English with several different words:
    Natural (1 Corinthians 2:14 KJV, NKJV, ESV; James 3:15 NAS; 1Corithinans 15:44, 46; both verses are translated as natural in every version of the Bible I saw)
    Sensual (James 3:15 KJV, NKJV; Jude 1:19 KJV)
    Worldly (Jude 1:19 NKJV, ESV)
    Unspiritual (James 3:15 ESV, NIV)
    Worldly-minded (Jude 1:19 NAS)
    Without the Spirit (1 Corinthians 2:14 NIV)
    Those who follow mere natural instincts (Jude 1:19 NIV)

19. 1 Peter 2:110

20. An interesting study of Psalms is to discover how the psalms of David are different from the psalms of Asaph, from the psalms of the sons of Korah, from psalms by Solomon, or Ethan the Ezraite, or Moses and any of the anonymous psalm composers. Look at the various topics, which categories the various songs may best fit, and how the different authors used language.

21. Years ago, a teaching on worship used animal characteristics to highlight worship styles, such as a lion and eagle. The teaching espoused style as pattern, which confused the issue.

22. In Pentecostal and Charismatic style churches, there is an attitude towards using music and songs as a catalyst for the Holy Spirit to move in the meeting. A false assumption underlies this mindset, of "setting the atmosphere" before the Holy Spirit will move. Jesus said, "where two or more are gathered in my name, there I am in the midst" (Matt. 18:20). Jesus is already there; we do not have to try to manipulate God or the congregation into an action. Ask God how your congregation should approach its time of music and song.

23. Chilvers, Ian, Osborne, Harold, and Farr, Dennis, ed., *The Oxford Dictionary of Art*, ©1994. Reproduced with permission of the Licensor through PLSclear. Page 267

24. I condense Tomas Kulka's *Kitsch and Art*, p. 80-82

25. Kulka, Tomas, *Kitsch and Art*, p. 73-74

26. M.-A. Couturier, *Sacred Art*, p.61

27. Kulka, Tomas, *Kitsch and Art*, p.27

28. De Mille, Agnes, *Portrait Gallery*, p.191

29. Plotinus, *The Enneads*, 1st Ennead, 6th Tractate: Beauty; reproduced in *What is Art? Aesthetic Theory From Plato to Tolstoy*, p. 80

30. Pope John Paul II, *Letter of His Holiness Pope John Paul II to Artists*, page 11

31. ibid, page 11

32. The label, "prophetic art" is not a good label. This label tries to cover topics not contained in the true sense of the word "prophetic"— as telling forth and foretelling. 1 Corinthians 12:4-11 gives a more specific breakdown. Starting in verse 4, it says, "There are diversities (or varieties) of gifts but the same Spirit (or Lord), there are differences (varieties) of services (ministries) but the same Lord, there are diversities (varieties) of activities but it is the same God who works all in all." Verse 7 explains, "To each is given the manifestation of the Spirit for the common good (profit of all). For to one is given through the Spirit the word (utterance, *logos*) of **wisdom** (ability, knowledge, *sophia*, with emphasis on applying the knowledge), and to another the *logos* of **knowledge**

(*gnosis*, knowledge of a special kind and relatively high in character) through the same Spirit, to another faith by the same Spirit, to another gifts of healing by the same Spirit, to another the working of miracles, to another **prophecy** (*propheteia*, predicting future events, a gifted faculty of setting forth and enforcing revealed truth), to another the ability to distinguish between spirits, to another various kinds of tongues, and to another the interpretation of tongues. All these are empowered by one and the same Spirit, distributing to each one individually as He wills."

An inspired Word of Wisdom, of Knowledge, and of Prophecy conveys how the Holy Spirit encourages us in our life and relationships, especially to Himself. Let us think in these terms specific to a biblical understanding of what is prophetic, not just a sloppy catch-all art label, called "prophetic".

33. *Peace Child* by Don Richardson, published by Regal Books, 1974, 2005
34. *The Discovery of Genesis: How the Truths of Genesis Were Found Hidden in the Chinese Language*, by C.H, Kang and Ethel R. Nelson, Concordia Publishing, 1979

❧ 7 ❧

THE PURPOSE OF IT ALL

Since before the year 2000, our culture has ignored the common understanding that Art expresses our human-ness. The new rationale supposes an audience, not a creator, supplies a work with meaning, be it a picture, movie, dance, play, song, story, or performance. We do not value a work for itself, as itself. Since society takes the stance that works are unfathomable, we place worth on works according to the emotions stirred; "how it makes us feel". If works are only the feelings they cause, we devour everything through our appetites and sugar rushes. Out of the "how it makes us feel" perspective, a question arose: "Are works knowable?" Artists, critics, curators, and other people of the arts have profusely discussed the "knowability" issue and explored another question: "Is Art a commodity for consumption?" Having been indoctrinated as a society in consumerism, we would answer yes and gobble up art.

COMMODITY

In the first part of this chapter, we will consider a generalized view of commodity, how Christians often approach it, and an opposing attitude. For most people, Art is unfathomable. Society teaches us to approach art based on the following primary indicators: who made the work and its price tag. But art's value is not reflected at its price point. In fact, monetary issues present a false view of works. Art's value stems from its expression of our humanity, not as an article of trade.

I observed consumer and commodity attitudes over the years and noticed we apply a similar mentality to our Christian journey, by assuming church activities function for our consumption. Pictures are used to convey messages or as decoration. Signs deliver information and direct consumers. We assess music by how it stroked our fancy this week, or failed to. We appraise the pastor's preaching by judging if they got to the point quick enough or if they stirred our emotions. The air made me cold. It was too hot. "People did not say 'hello,' so they must not like me." Such exclamations are indicators we view and place value on church as consumers.

Do we go to church to gorge on the performance through our stirred-up emotions? Yes. Preachers and music leaders may feel forced to become performers for the consumer-congregation instead of leading us before God. The commodity dogma evangelizes a consumption message through branding. People caught in the consumption trap must recognize how society shaped their attitudes to devour products, including chasing leaders viewed as a better brand. The need for titles reinforces commodified branding.

My encapsulation of the commodity rationale is this: an unrenewed mind. Jesus addressed consumerist attitudes in many ways. One instance was at The Last Supper; Jesus told the disciples that to become leaders like him, they were to follow his example of being a servant. Then he washed their feet, which was low and unglorified. A servant does not consume but serves. Service is not about our wants or how we feel, but looks at how the needs of others can be met.

There are many excellent books covering our commodified attitudes and consumption mentality, so I need not continue. A great introduction to a commodity perspective regarding the arts, and for an overall view on commodity, is a documentary by a former Time magazine art critic Robert Hughes (1938-2012): *The Mona Lisa Curse* (2008).[1]

GIFTS

Kester Brewin, a writer and public theologian, sees the opposite of commodity is a gift.[2] We give gifts without expecting something in return. If a gift has strings attached, it is an exchange or payment. I noticed a gift outlook addresses many issues a commodity attitude cannot fulfill.

The gift viewpoint is an underlying concept throughout the New Testament. When the term "gift" is used, it has two different emphases, one being an object or service given to someone, and the second being what God has placed inside a person as an ability or a way of looking at life.

Let us first touch on a generalized biblical view of gifts.

- "Christ's gift," as Paul described in Ephesians 4:7, is the first gift Christians consider. Paul talks several times in Ephesians about Jesus' gift to us. In brief, God gave Jesus to us as a gift of salvation. To benefit from Christ's salvation, we must take hold of the gift. "If you confess with your mouth that Jesus is Lord and believe in your heart that God raised him from the dead, you will be saved" (Romans 10:9). An excellent summary of Jesus' gift is Titus 3:5, "he saved us, not because of works done by us in righteousness, but according to his own mercy, by the washing of regeneration and renewal of the Holy Spirit." I also like Ephesians 2:8-9, "For by grace you have been saved through faith. And this is not of your own doing; it is a gift of God, not a result of works so that no one may boast." St. Paul in Ephesians includes Gentiles as co-heirs (3:6). God's gift of salvation through Jesus is for Jews and also the non-Jew. Beyond salvation, God adopts us into his family. Now, we have an inheritance sealed with the Holy Spirit as a guarantee (Ephesians 1:3-14).

- God gave gifts to the Church. Ephesians 4:11-12, "The gifts he *gave* were that some would be apostles, some prophets, some evangelists, some pastors, and teachers, to equip the saints for the work of the ministry, for building up the body of Christ." These gifts from God come in the form of persons exercising service-work as servant-ministers.

- We often forget God places us with people and in situations as a gift for someone else's life. Paul and Silas were gifts for the Philippian jailer (Acts 16:9-34), Mark, the cousin of Barnabas, was useful to Paul (2 Tim. 4:11); Stephanas, Fortunatus, and Achaicus refreshed Paul's spirit (1 Cor. 16:17-18), Philemon refreshed the saints (Philemon 1:4-7), and we could find many more examples throughout the New Testament.

- God gave to each person many "gifts that differ according to the grace given to us" (Romans 12:6). Let us use them. When we are born, we have unlimited potential in our being. Our gifts reveal themselves as we grow up, but we may or may not develop them.

As we grow older, the openness to develop and realize our gifts shrinks. However, Christians shouldn't settle for this natural tendency. We can choose to move beyond our soulish comfort by putting off the old man and putting on Christ (Romans 13:14; Colossians 3:1-17). We are not to stop at a certain point of maturity with God. The individuals who remain receptive to God's leading grow in Christ, releasing greater potential. Because we continually grow, others receive God's love and hope. As the parable of the talents illustrates, the gifts and talents the master gives us, he expects us to use, not entomb. Have we embraced the enemy's lies that our gifts are not good, or talent skipped us? If so, we suppress and censor our treasures.

Additional gift-abilities may develop after we use a preceding gift. For instance, we learn to speak in the first couple of years after we are born. The language center of our brain grows and increases through use, to process, then imprint the words and language structure into our mind. After we learn to speak, we learn to write words. The actions of writing transform another area of the brain using gross motor activities for the arm and hand, then later fine motor skills developed with our fingers. Through writing, our mind associates a movement's stroke with a letter, connecting several strokes to form a word. Many strokes link to make sentences.

A deaf person first connects physical actions to words and letters because this is how they initially use language. When they learn to read and write, the letters and words on the page join to the meaning of the signs they already know and employ. As God has given each person creative talents and spiritual gifts, we develop them through use, and grow from there.

GIFT DYNAMICS

To better understand gifts, let us break apart the action of giving a gift. Giving has three parts. The first component of giving is the offering of something. The second component is what is being offered. Third is the receiving of the thing being offered.

Have you seen someone refuse a gift? Maybe the person perceived the gift was really an exchange, such as sitting through a time-share presentation for a "gift-pass" to Walt Disney World. Another reason people do not receive gifts, they may dislike the humility they feel when another person gives to them. This kind of personal barrier might refuse God and his many gifts. Or a person may receive a gift from God, like forgiveness, but then withhold it from others.

Gift giving has at its core some type of relationship, from a surface association to a deep, lasting one. Often there is an established connection with the person to whom you give a gift. A link may also stem from proximity: a person is nearby, and we offer them something, even though we never met before, such as giving a stranger a coupon in a coffee shop or grocery store.

Jesus, who knew us from before the foundation of the world, gave his life for us while we were yet strangers and sinners. Christ's gift was relational. We were clueless and did not perceive Jesus' precious gift, but now, having freely received God's gifts, we can also freely give (Matthew 10:8).

SHARING GIFTS

Children enjoy presenting gifts; they understand gifts are for giving. Children take pleasure in distributing something they made, such as a drawing we will put on a refrigerator. Children may offer a picture, a story, a dance, a song, playing music on an instrument, or a rock they found while playing. Children love to give, particularly when they personally invest in the sharing.

As adults, we can continue to give gifts to people. Our sharing flows from God's character and is part of God's image in us. When we accept Christ, we take on His divine nature in a continual divine exchange[3] with our human nature. We convey God's giving disposition just as we do God's creative temperament.

THE NORMAL CHURCH OUTLETS

Let us examine how we share our gifts and abilities in our local church community. As you survey the aesthetic interactions that surround you, observe how we mix Christian consumerism with the way we follow the Holy Spirit's leading at stewarding our gifts.

In a typically structured congregation, there is a leader, often called pastor. The pastor may or may not be part of the ruling/overseeing group, often called board of directors, elders, leadership council, or another term. There is an office with office workers. Someone cleans the building and maintains the facility. There are several areas of service with which people may connect: youth and kids, home groups, music, greeters, ushers, audio/visual. We may serve by teaching adult and children's Sunday School classes. Sick people and widows require visiting. The poor and homeless have many needs. A church may have evangelism teams. There is prayer and intercession. Many churches are involved with missions. And congregations may have other areas for ministry. We have many ways to contribute. I encourage you to serve in the aforementioned areas if you do not already.

Creative people have extra conduits to share their gifts. Singers may sing in a choir or through special music. Musicians may play in the worship band or for specific presentations. Some churches at Christmas or Easter may do a dramatic performance. Church leaders often control the congregation's abilities, assuming wild talents must conform to approved outlets. Is this a correct approach?

Overall, churches provide two approaches for people to contribute: one is keeping the workings of a church running, and the other is to make each meeting the best meeting we can achieve. I recognize other service areas, like evangelism or visiting the sick and poor, that take us from a building and meeting. When we work the services out-of-the-building, do we emphasize people should go to a meeting?

Churches seem to highlight assemblies. Sometimes God shows up in a gathering. We often assume the only place the Holy Spirit performs is in our meetings. God has mercy on us, manifesting His love through the congregation's meeting until quenched. But I would like to make an important point: God also displays His love and hope outside a congregational assembly. I believe God joins us outside the public meetings more than in them. The Holy Spirit is with us when we get together casually over coffee. In Matthew 18:20, Jesus said, "For where two or three are gathered in my name, there I am in the midst of them." As we are God's representatives, we can expect miracles through such everyday happenings.

MEETINGS

The traditional church approach trained us to consume a handful of people's skills in a meeting, along with judging the effects of their gift usage. As consumers, we make judgments about whatever we devour; therefore, you may hear phrases like, "The music was good today" or "The preaching was right on point." We expect a meeting will meet our needs, then label it good or bad accordingly. Since we gulp down meetings, we dislike changes which take us out of our comfort zone. And, if someone sits in our spot, we strongly disapprove!

Our consumption attitude influences how we experience church, even frames our Christian experience. We imagine an assembly will fulfill our cravings, like going to a restaurant, expecting whatever we gobble down will satisfy. But church meetings cannot complete us, only Jesus can. Do we reason that church meetings and Jesus are equal?

DISSATISFACTION

Let us continue and glance at one aspect of the Christian growth process which influences how we express creative works. Churches are good at helping a new Christian grow in Christ. This is one of its strengths. Yet in the maturing process, there comes a stage when dissatisfaction arises, which becomes a juncture point, either for maturity or the enemy uses to turn individuals away from the faith. From a place of discontent, people often switch churches, looking for a place that will "feed" them. Most people think the agitation they feel is because of needed changes to meetings or preaching styles or music, or some other surface issue. The accuser uses dissatisfaction to make us question our faith and the basis of our beliefs. Questioning beliefs is not bad, as we can use it to ensure our beliefs are on solid rock instead of shifting ground.

When I was in my twenties, I heard people from my church, and other congregations, expressed restlessness with the church experience. Through the exclamations of those around me, I noticed dissatisfaction is a natural part of the maturing process. Dissatisfaction is a good sign; it shows we are growing up. What works for children is unfulfilling for adults. During the transition, those who embrace spiritual maturity perceive that the purpose for church is to give—to God and to people—not go to get. If people do not have a maturing revelation, they will continue in their childish church consumption, expecting everyone else to meet their needs and soulish desires. Growing up in Christ means we are not to remain as babies. The arising dissatisfaction pushes people to take action. Most of the time, people's action is to jump to another church, expecting the next church will satisfy their consumption. When the new church does not mollify the frustration, they skip to another church, and then another, and so on. In this scenario, the immature individual places responsibility for growing up in Christ on everyone else's shoulders instead of their own. During this time, the accuser speaks unbelief to their mind, along with whatever lies the person *will* believe, so that they become unstable. Therefore, we may hear how people turn away from Jesus, even when they are leaders.

When we congregate in our buildings for a meeting (*ekklēsia* —Greek; gathering, assembly, congregation, church), do we limit God to our ways? Yes. And we assume God will work through our arrangements. Churches operate either through a tight-style or open-style structure. There is value in both methodologies, and they both share the same weakness when rigidity to the form disregards the Holy Spirit's promptings. I acknowledge many churches seek to break from the locked forms in either arrangement, to desiring greater openness with the Holy Spirit in whatever way that means.

Our present church system does not help people grow past a middle school level of maturity. To give the benefit of the doubt, there may be churches that are exceptions to this. I hope many, many churches are beyond my estimation. So, the immature goes to church to have their needs met. This is good for babies and children. As individuals mature, they realize they must help others in their needs. When creative people express each stage of growth, it is important that they find the freedom and the value in connecting with others through ways not locked in rigidity.

HOW CHURCHES APPROACH THE ARTS

Church culture acknowledges the dissatisfaction, which may have pushed many churches to include the arts in church life. Our idea of how we *ecclesia*—be the church—determines the way we give our abilities. Congregations manage the arts in two ways. One approach is using the arts interactively in meetings: video presentations, skits, music, art on the walls, dance presentations, drawing or painting a picture during a meeting, etc. We desire to make the meeting be the best meeting we can make. The arts are used to reinforce the belief that the church-is-the-meeting. The other method uses the arts as a tool to reach or engage the community through art galleries, presenting plays and musicals, making movies, or holding concerts.

A supplement to the church-is-the-meeting, is church-is-a-building. For the Christian, the building is a place of contemplation; and for the non-Christian, it is an attraction or curiosity. The church-is-the-building point of view is a holdover from a medieval understanding of church, where design and decoration speak of God's salvation and deliverance. Today, many traditional churches, such as Catholic, Lutheran, Anglican, etc., often feature various pointers to God's redemption throughout their buildings. In contrast, less traditional churches may view certain forms of art in a church setting as idolatrous. Therefore, church is the meeting. The building is a shell, which is often ugly or bland. We assume meetings are the pearl in the shell. Church leaders use the arts to highlight what is important—the meeting.

Another model church culture employs art for, as a tool to connect with the community outside the church building. In this approach, evangelism is the underlying motive. As noted above, many churches hosted exhibitions, have an art gallery, churches present plays and musicals, a few make movies, and some hold concerts. There are books about starting an "art ministry" which is primarily aimed at beginner and amateur artists, Christian or non-Christian.[4]

The weakness of each method is the assumption the arts must present specific messages. We consider the message the most important thing because we consume it, but a message is not the work. How many times have you heard, "It is not what you say, but how you say it?" If the message is all we convey without considering how we express it, we fall into what the Bible calls "bearing false witness". A false witness is someone who misrepresents, whether on purpose or by accident. Moses is an example; God would not let Moses enter the Promised Land because, in his frustration and anger with the people, Moses misrepresented God to them when they were at Meribah—the place where water gushed out of the rock (Numbers 20:1-13). I observed that our biases in church and our culturally ingrained presumptions about life often slant the way we share Jesus, which is often inaccurate.

To use the arts truly, we make works that are *more* than a message. We articulate the idea in such a way to bring out its fullness—of thought, expression, significance, and life. Consider the way Psalms, Proverbs, Ecclesiastes, Song of Songs, and even Job express a vast array of ideas.

God is Creator and put creativity into our being. Every Christian is an ambassador, representing and reflecting the fullness of

God's Kingdom. Let us ensure we are a true witness, not just a message marketer or propaganda pusher.

IS A WORK IN BALANCE?

When we share our creative workings, how may we understand the effects of our works; its witness, so to speak? We observe where the weight of a work concentrates. Imagine a work as a balancing scale, one arm holding its idea/content, and the other arm holding the content's expression. When the weight is wholly on a Message, the work is off balance, perceived as only propaganda. If the weight is primarily Expression, this is decoration. Decoration does not have enough sustaining substance to keep us interested. When the weight of a work is balanced between Content and its Expressed manner, we want to interact with it longer. Next, we check if a synergizing dynamic energy infuses the work. We identify works that have a dynamic-vital energy as "good".

This quick review over the topics of Chapter Three reminds us a work's weight placement determines how we convey an idea, which helps us understand objectively its witness to others. If we want God's Spirit to infuse life through our actions, our works need to contain a balanced symphonic-harmonious dynamic between its Content and Expression. Most of the time, we assume the message is all that matters. But, this thinking is lop-sided. Synergy cannot generate in an imbalanced work. Presenting the truth of God significantly through our creative talents and skills leaves an imprint on an audience, because the presentation is as important as the *what* presented. Jesus understood this; look at how he presented different themes through parables, such as the kingdom of God, forgiveness, prayer, and faith. When we follow significance like Jesus did, we share the Holy Spirit's inspirations through our works.

LOGOS AND RHEMA

To study the synergy between a Content and its Expression, we can parallel the dealings of Greek concepts *logos* and *rhema*; both translate to English as "word". Let us investigate their underlying interaction.

Logos is the full counsel of God, the total eternal expression-representation of God, the word of God, message, subject matter; it is a generalized term.

> *In the beginning was the Word (logos), and the Word (logos) was with God, and the Word (logos) was God.*

> John 1:1

> *And the Word (logos) became flesh and dwelt among us...*

> John 1:14

Rhema is a present tense action associated with *logos*; it is a word-direction. In the New Testament, it relates to the Holy Spirit enlivening a present-now inspiration-action of *logos,* which directs an individual.

> *But what does it say? 'The word [rhema] is near you, in your mouth and your heart' (that is the word [rhema] of faith that we proclaim).*

> Romans 10:8

Logos (as a general term for God's Full Word, its message, or subject) bonds with *rhema* (the inspired application for *logos)* which brings to life whatever the Holy Spirit highlights in a personalized and directing manner. *Rhema* affects in a specific, directional way, and we can then see how the animated something is articulated in our life now, i.e., as Expression. The Holy Spirit may also activate his *rhema* through what we do, as it falls in line with *logos*. Are our works such that the Holy Spirit would enliven them? Sadly, not most of the time.

PSALMS, HYMNS, AND SPIRITUAL SONGS

People are fascinated when we express Holy Spirit inspiration, more so when *rhema* synergizes our works' expression. The Apostle Paul advised the church at Ephesus on how to articulate the Holy Spirit's stimulations. He said in Ephesians 5:18-19, "...be filled with the Spirit, speaking to one another in psalms and hymns and spiritual songs, singing and making melody in your heart to the Lord".

Let's look at Paul's categories.

- *Psalms* are songs set to music (Greek *psalmos,* a song set to music).
- *Hymns* are more specifically songs praising God (Greek *hymnos*, a song of praise where a song's prominent thought is the praise of God).
- *Spiritual songs* are songs of how God relates to us and influences our lives (Greek *pneumatik*, spiritual, pertaining to spirits, relating to the influences of the Holy Spirit. From this word, we get our English word "pneumatic," which means air-powered). In general, we say these songs are about the Holy Spirit powering our lives.
- *Singing and making melody to the Lord with your heart.* "Singing" is to give voice musically (Greek *adō*, meaning to sing). "Making melody" (Greek word *psallō*, means to strike the strings or chords of an instrument; to sing to music). Striking a string

produces a vibration on the string; the vibration travels along the string to resonate the sound through a sound box, which is how we hear the sound-vibration. When we give voice to the melody God vibrates in our heart and present it to the Lord and to other people, they receive its benefit.

Basically, Paul said we are to be filled with God's Spirit and speak to each other through the way God interacts with us and guides our life. We best communicate God's Spirit through creative gifts, as Paul's categories show. This ancient truth is for us today, as we consider how to share God's inspirations with those around us.

EPHESIANS 5:14-19

When using our creative talents, we do not just slap elements together, hoping something turns out; we reflect our Creator. We organize our ideas through some type of compositional arrangement that best expresses what we want to convey. We should understand the way we transmit an idea is as important as the concept itself. The Holy Spirit enlivens an idea through its expression.

So, let us meditate on the following Scriptures.

> *"Awake, O sleeper, and arise from the dead, and Christ will shine on you." Look carefully then how you walk, not as unwise but as wise, making the best use of the time, because the days are evil. Therefore do not be foolish, but understand what the will of the Lord is. And do not get drunk with wine, for that is debauchery, but be filled with the Spirit, addressing one another in psalms and hymns and spiritual songs, singing and making melody to the Lord with your heart...*

Ephesians 5:14-19

Paul tells us in these verses to make the best use of time. How do we do this? We wake up to understand the will of the Lord and walk in it. God freely gave to us, and we can give to others; not from our soul-strength, but through the Holy Spirit's *rhema*. We must not be foolish by gravitating to feeling-orientated habits, like having too much wine. Debauchery is intemperate consumption or a lack of self-control. But Paul directs us to first be filled with the Spirit. If we do not pass on God's Spirit, we will only give our assumptions and judgments of people and their situations, which surface as accusations and condemnation. When we continually receive the Holy Spirit's power, we share Christ's life as the Holy Spirit directs, touching other's needs through our gifts, even our creative gifts.

WHEN WE COME TOGETHER

Christ shed his blood, died on the cross, then resurrected—and for what? For all humanity. And more intimately, each one of us personally. When we accept Jesus, we receive his spirit and power and are complete in Christ.[5] Now we share as God's ambassadors, which means we represent God to others. Since we are ambassadors, representative of God's kingdom, we must ready ourselves. Let us understand, everywhere we go, God's kingdom is. When we share our gifts and talents as the Holy Spirit inspires and directs, we reflect God's character of creativity, giving, power, and love.[6]

As you are God's representative, be ready to give voice to the Holy Spirit's vibration (hope) resonating in you. How should we express God's rhythms and beats? Maybe in the manner the Apostle Paul stated in 1 Corinthians 14:26, "What then brothers? When you come together, each one has a hymn, a lesson, a revelation, a tongue, or an interpretation. Let all things be done for building up." We are to prepare ourselves to disclose the Holy

Spirit's images; that is the essence of this Scripture, both for inside a meeting and out of one. Are we willing to share our gifts as the verse directs? If so, we operate similarly to jazz improvisation. Have you seen a group of jazz musicians improvise? Improvisation is not a free-for-all. I heard Ellis Marsalis (1934-2020, a jazz pianist, teacher/mentor, and father of several musicians) speak about improvisation at an art conference. It was wonderful listening to Ellis Marsalis. He said musicians must know a song inside out before they improvise with it. Musicians use the song as a base structure. Improvisation follows a melody, jumping off the song as inspiration leads, but will return, never really leaving. Each musician must listen closely to the other musicians' contributions so they may add their own insight without sounding like they are off on their own. The musicians doing their own thing are described as "selfish" as they do not listen to the song, the inspiration around the song, nor to other musicians' inspired contributions. The musicians playing together recognize when someone does *not* follow inspiration.

I think of improvisation like a Christmas tree. The tree provides the structure and support for the ornaments, garlands, and lights. The song is the tree, and musicians may give a lot of ornament but never really leave the song. Listening to Ellis Marsalis speak, I remembered 1 Corinthians 14:26. Paul essentially described jazz improvisation almost 1800 years before jazz existed, saying that when we come together, we should follow the Holy Spirit's improvisation, becoming so sensitive we can spot whether someone is out on their own or following the Holy Spirit's direction and sharing God's life. When a person does their own thing, drawing attention away from the Holy Spirit's direction, we discern the selfishness and recognize the disorder. We must finely tune ourselves to the Holy Spirit's flow through us and through others, testing the contribution, letting mistakes occur, but correcting whatever disrupts the flow, so an individual develops a mature sensitivity to the Holy Spirit's improvisational guidance.

The argument against applying 1 Corinthians 14:26 today is taken from 1 Corinthians 14:33a, "For God is not a God of confusion but of peace," and 1 Corinthians 14:40, "But, all things should be done decently and in order."[7] Most people assume order is about control, of time and people, to regulate the Holy Spirit's revelations. We misunderstand "order" as structural control: do this, then this, and not this, until time is up. Our controls may lead to manipulating people.

Maybe the people imposing order are terrible listeners, or are too "selfish" to hear what others contribute, or do not perceive the orderliness of improvisation, or perhaps they simply do not work well with others. People may come together but not follow the Holy Spirit's inspiration and direction, which is the reason for confusion. When we follow the Holy Spirit's lead in sharing our gifts, others receive God's love. Developing God's gifts (including our creative gifts) entails operating at higher levels of responsibility. In doing so, we put away childish ways.

THE WRAP-UP

The Holy Spirit is creative and relates to us on this level. The arts, as a physical expression of the soul and spirit, best express how the Holy Spirit interacts with us. And when we share an inspired work's significance (*rhema*), people often have profound encounters.

God put us (representative of His Kingdom) with other people to be a gift of God to them. If we do not access God's Spirit, we confine ourselves to our own opinion; as did the person I described in the Introduction, whose judgments condemned me, killing the relationship I had with their family. God's Spirit brings life. If you wonder if you truly communicate God's messages to people, check the result. Have others' lives gone deeper with God, or did relationships end? We know we follow the Holy Spirit's leading when God's life is evident through our actions and in the results.

Therefore, the purpose of it all is to share God's life and love with others as the Holy Spirit directs us through our gifts, even our creative gifts. Let me encourage you from 2 Timothy 1:6-7, "For this reason I remind you to fan into flame the gift of God, which is in you…for God gave us a spirit not of fear but of power and love and self-control." And finally, from Hebrews 10:24, "let us consider one another, in order to stir up love and good works".

---

1. Hughes, Robert, *The Mona Lisa Curse*, Oxford Film and Television for Channel 4, UK, 2008. You can watch this on YouTube.
2. Brewin, Kester, *Signs of Emergence: A Vision for Church That Is Organic/Networked/Decentralized/Bottom-up/Communal/Flexible/Always Evolving*, Baker Books, 2007
3. The divine exchange is not a one-time action but happens throughout our life.
4. Organizations like Christians in the Visual Arts are geared towards professional artists. Chaiya Art Awards in England recognizes artists who successfully explore spirituality and faith. There is a growing availability of works on Christian themes. This is good. The increased availability of Christian themed works also makes it more important that we not just accept everything as good work because of its message but test each work, even to challenge artists to go deeper at conveying God's Truth and Love.
5. Colossians 2:9-10 "For in Him dwells all the fullness of the Godhead bodily; and you are complete in Him, who is the head of all principality and power."
6. 2 Timothy 4:2
7. 1 Corinthians 14:39 says, "So, my brothers, earnestly desire to prophesy, and do not forbid speaking in tongues." This verse is the sentence immediately preceding vs. 40, "But all things should be done decently and in order." We can see how vs. 40 is taken out of context and misapplied to fit a preconceived notion, i.e., an individual's pretext. Verse 39 goes back to the point, of sharing God's *rhema* images.

CONCLUSION

We covered a lot of ground in this book. Should we contemplate anything else? Yes. Here is the last point to ponder: "What aspiration do we have for our works?" God has an intended aim for His works. Isaiah 55:11 clearly states this point: "so shall my word be that goes out from my mouth; it shall not return to me empty, but shall accomplish that which I purpose, and shall succeed in the thing for which I sent it." Messages by themselves do not have life. God's life goes out through his Word (*logos* and *rhema*).

I will share an incident which clarified this point for me. In 1994, I traveled with my father around Italy and Switzerland. This was my first trip to both countries. I experienced several key significant moments in Rome: seeing the Sistine Chapel, the Roman ruins, and drawing the Coliseum. One afternoon at a Baptist church, I met a troupe from the non-denominational mission training organization, Youth With A Mission (YWAM). The troupe went to Central America before coming to Europe and danced a dramatic dance in the countries visited. That evening, the YWAM group performed their dramatic dance at the Piazza Navona for a street presentation. I arrived almost two hours before the group and passed the time sketching an Italian man near me and the fountain Bernini (1598-1680, sculptor/architect) made for the center of the piazza. I sat with local Italians when the YWAM troupe delivered their dance.

Several people from the local church came with the troupe to talk with people after the presentation. Following the dance performance, an Italian man sitting next to me got into a heated argument with a man that accompanied the YWAM troupe. I listened to their fiery exclamations for several minutes, then asked the man next to me what they were discussing. He told me, in English, the troupe's arrogance offended him, and the dance patronizing.

I agreed with the Italian man as he expressed his view, but for a different reason. Meeting the group earlier, I heard what they did in Central America and their heart's desire that God use them to touch people with His life. I believe the patronizing effect the Italian man detected was from a cultural difference unknown to the YWAM troupe as they presented the dance. The places in Central America they visited were of 2nd and 3rd World conditions, mostly 3rd World, and the presentation was appropriate for that cultural climate. Rome is a 1st World culture. Italians developed and cultivated their society to understand the arts, since history covers centuries of art development in Italy. Most Italians are sensitive to many nuances of the arts. So, when the group performed the 3rd World presentation in a 1st World environment, the 1st World's reception did not match the 3rd World's. The Romans looked at the dance with greater understanding because of a thorough awareness with the medium. The Italian man sitting next to me understood the message, in the way they showed it, and the conveyance upset him more than any agreement or disagreement with the message.

I see the incident representative of the way we approach the arts. The YWAM troupe came, danced in Italy, and left without grasping the audience's reception. They probably only considered the message's acceptance or rejection. The local Christians had to manage the fall-out. When we are unaware how an audience will receive our work, we only spout out a message, being clueless to what we communicate. We fail to share God's life.

We should also grasp how an audience may interpret our works. People interpret works through various worldviews. Recognition of worldviews assists a maker constructing works to clarify their intent intentionally. Any dissents should come from disagreements with ideas, not shoddy expressions to the idea.

To enter the Land of The Arts, let us realize just making something is not good enough. "Good enough" may work at church, but not to a culturally/artistically informed audience. We are to understand our audience. We are not propagating messages to the masses. We share, as a witness, what we see and experience. Let us include in our witness, relaying the questions of life we ponder on and ask God about because these questions (and many more besides) artists consider and explore through their work. Through our communications, we articulate the Holy Spirit's revelations and life in power, love, and self-control—skillfully.

The enemy has done an outstanding job confusing us about creativity. We often devalue our expressions and withhold sharing the Holy Spirit's promptings. Let us leave the confusion behind. "For God is not a God of confusion but of peace" (1 Corinthians 14:33). And we should apply Hebrews 6:1 to our current perception of the arts: "Therefore, let us leave behind the elementary doctrines of Christ and go on to maturity, not laying again a foundation of repentance from dead works and of faith towards God...". As we apply this verse to our works, we go on to maturity, through creative labors, along with testing ours and other's results.

To boil it all down, the Church's response is as witness of God's significant creative-ness placed inside each person, reflecting the wonder of the Creator's image throughout the universe, shown in our lives, expressed through our works.

SOME REMINDERS:

To conclude the conclusion, let us recap a few highlights.

- From the time we are born, everyone shows God's creative character. Our creativity flows out of who we are. It is not about what we do. I want to emphasize it is a manifestation of God's image that permeates and flows out of our innermost being.
- The Bible does not condemn creative undertakings and its ensuing works, i.e., art, unless we turn it into our source. Christian condemnation of the arts stems from a Sacred/Secular mindset, where a biblical judgment of idolatry is misinterpreted for an overall disapproval towards the arts. Christians seeking to regulate contamination are *not* sharing God's love.
- Remember, we have a ministry of reconciliation, first with ourselves and then with others.
- Check if a work conveys significance and life? If not, are the works cliché, trivial, sterile? The beauty and depth of God's life is not a cliché, but relevant to our whole being and place in the world. Therefore, ask yourself, "Do the works we prefer reflect the substance and deepness of God's life? Or do we choose for ourselves echoes of society's superficiality?"
- Test works. Examine how an Expression relays its Content. Recall that testing does not judge a Content's morality. Moral stances shut-down conversations with artists, because our judgments condemn them, and their creative actions. Judging blocks people's reconciliation to God.
- We have believed society's indoctrination: creativity and its expressions are unimportant. Our moral

stances about the arts minimize the works and its makers. Creative people persevere through the public's misunderstanding, wrong judgments, and hostile attitudes towards them and their work. So, if you want a proper conversation, discuss the way a work's Content is Expressed, and did the maker fully Express the idea. When a maker has this type of conversation, they may open up and share their intentions for the work, even if they did not pull it off. Here, we begin the ministry of reconciliation.

Keep in mind Jesus' words:

You are the salt of the earth, but if salt has lost its taste, how shall its saltiness be restored? It is no longer good for anything except to be thrown out and trampled under people's feet. You are the light of the world. A city set on a hill cannot be hidden.

Matthew 5:13-14

———

You *are* salt. You *are* light. You will affect people because you are there, even without speaking. And, when you communicate, remember you are God's representative—ambassador of His agape, His life.

Go and share God's life, even through your works.

APPENDIX

HEBREW AND GREEK WORDS FOR "WORK" IN THE BIBLE

In case you are interested, listed below are the Hebrew and Greek words for "work".

In looking at the Hebrew and Greek words for "work," we see there are two basic uses: as a verb—the action of doing work, and as a noun—the result of the working action, the thing. Included in the definitions of the Greek words is the energy needed for the work.

- Hebrew *dabar* - word, matter (like any event), thing; Psalm 145:5; Ecclesiastes 10:12
- Hebrews *yagia* - labor, heavy work, the result of labor, produce, gain; Job 10:3
- Hebrew *yad* - hand, power, strength, direction, care; Exodus 14:31
- Hebrew *yēṣer* - something formed, creation, inclination, disposition, motivation; Habakkuk 2:18
- Hebrew *m'la'kah* - work, labor, deed, duty, craft, service; thing, something made, something done (This

is used in relation to God's work and Man's work.);
Genesis 2, 3, 4, 5, 39; Exodus 1, 5, 7, 12, 14, 20, 23,
25, 26, 28, 31, 32, 34, 35, 36, 37, 38, 39, 40; Leviticus
23; Numbers 8, 10, 16, 23, 28, 29, 31; Deuteronomy
2, 3, 4, 5, 11, 14, 15, 16, 21, 24, 28, 30, 31, 32, 33;
Joshua 24; Judges 2, 5, 13, 19; Ruth 2; 1 Samuel 8, 11,
14, 19, 25; 2 Samuel 23, 24; 1 Kings 5, 6, 7, 9, 16; 2
Kings 5, 12, 19, 22; 1 Chronicles 6, 9, 16, 21, 22, 23,
25, 26, 27, 28, 28; 2 Chronicles 2, 3, 4, 5, 8, 15, 16, 24,
29, 30, 31, 32, 34; Ezra 2, 3, 4, 5, 6; Nehemiah 2, 4, 5,
6, 7, 9, 10, 11, 13; Job 1, 10, 14, 23, 34, 36, 37, 40;
Psalm 8, 9, 17, 28, 31, 33, 46, 53, 59, 62, 68, 73, 74,
77, 78, 86, 88, 90, 92, 95, 96, 98, 101, 102, 103, 104,
105, 106, 107, 111, 115, 119, 135, 138, 139, 141, 143,
145; Proverbs 18, 24; Jeremiah 17, 18, 48, 50; Ezekiel
15, 28; Haggia 1

- Hebrew *mabad* - deed, action, doing; Job 34:25;
  Daniel 4:37

- Hebrew *ma'aliyl* - an act, deed; Psalm 77, 78;
  Nehemiah 9:35

- Hebrew *ma'aśeh* - work, deed, labor, doing, act,
  something made, something done; Genesis 5; Exodus
  5, 18, 23, 24, 26, 28, 32, 34, 36, 37, 39, 30; Numbers
  8, 16, 31; Deuteronomy 2, 3, 4, 14, 15, 16, 24, 27, 28,
  30, 31; Joshua 24; Judges 2, 19; 1 Samuel 8, 19; 1
  Kings 7, 13, 16; 2 Kings 16, 19, 22; 1 Chronicle 23; 2
  Chronicles 3, 4, 20, 31, 32, 34; Nehemiah 6; Job 1,
  14, 34, 37; Psalm 8, 19, 28, 33, 62, 66, 86, 90, 92, 102,
  103, 104, 106, 107, 111, 115, 118, 135, 138, 139, 143,
  145; Proverbs 16, 31; Ecclesiastes 1, 2, 3, 4, 5, 7, 8, 9,
  11, 12; Song of Solomon 7; Isaiah 2, 5, 10, 17, 19, 26,
  28, 29, 32, 37, 41, 54, 57, 59, 60, 64, 65, 66; Jeremiah
  1, 7, 10, 25, 32, 44, 48, 51; Lamentations 3, 4; Ezekiel
  1, 6, 16, 46; Daniel 9; Hosea 13, 14; Amos 8; Jonah 3;
  Micah 5, 6; Haggai 2

- Hebrew *mip'āl* - work, deed, doing, act, acts; Psalm 46:8, 66:4, Proverbs 8:22
- Hebrew *ma'aśeh* - work, labor, deed, act, something made, something done; Exodus 5:3, Psalm 66, Ecclesiastes 9:10
- Hebrew *abad* - a deed, what is done, doing, act, service; Ecclesiastes 9:1
- Hebrew *'aḇoḏāh* - work, service, labor, task, duty, job, special work or service to God; forced labor, slavery; Exodus 5, 39; Numbers 4; Nehemiah 3
- Hebrew *'aḇiyḏāh* - work, service, deed, administration; Ezra 4, 5, 6
- Hebrew *'alyilāh* what is done, deed, act, action; Psalm 14, 78, 141
- Hebrew *'aliliyyāh* - act, action, deed; Jeremiah 32:19
- Hebrew *poal* - work, deed, doing, labor; Deuteronomy 32, 33; Ruth 2; Job 7, 24, 34, 36; Psalm 9, 44, 64, 77, 90, 92, 95, 104, 111, 143; Proverbs 20, 21, 24; Isaiah 5, 41, 45; Jeremiah 25, 50; Habakkuk 1, 3
- Hebrew *p'ullāh* - work, deed, recompense; 2 Chronicles 15; Psalm 17, 28; Proverbs 11; Isaiah 40, 49, 61, 62, 65; Jeremiah 31

———

- Greek *energeia* - energy, in working; Ephesians 1, 3, 4; Philippians 3; Colossians 1; 2 Thessalonians 2
- Greek *energema* - an energy, in working; 1 Corinthians 12
- Greek *ergasia* - work, business, gain; Ephesians 4
- Greek *ergazomai* - to work, labor, do, perform, produce to trade, traffic, do business; to act, exert one" power, be active, commit, to be engaged in, occupied upon, acquire, gain by one" labor; Matthew

21, 25, 26; Luke 13; John 5, 6; 1 Corinthians 9; Revelations 18

- Greek *ergon* - a work, deed, business, action, anything done or to be done, a product of an action or process; Matthew 5, 11, 23, 26; Mark 13, 14; John 4, 5, 6, 7, 8, 9, 10, 14, 15, 17; Acts 5, 7, 9, 13, 14, 15, 26; Romans 2, 3, 4, 9, 11, 13, 14; 1 Corinthians 3, 9, 15, 16; 2 Corinthians 9, 11; Galatians 2, 3, 5, 6; Ephesians 2, 4, 5; Philippians 1, 2; Colossians 1; 1 Thessalonians 1, 5; 2 Thessalonians 1, 2; 1 Timothy 2, 3, 5, 6; 2 Timothy 1, 2, 3, 4; Titus 1, 2, 3; Hebrews 1, 2, 3, 4, 6, 9, 10, 13; James 1, 2, 3; 1 Peter 1, 2; 2 Peter 3; 1 John 3; Revelation 2, 3, 9, 14, 15, 20, 22
- Greek *logos* - word, a thing uttered, matter, speech, discourse, expression, form of words, message, account, report, narrative, reason, treatise, doctrine, plea, motive, the Word of God, the full Word of God, the divine Word; Romans 9
- Greek *pragma* - anything done, affair; James 3
- Greek *praxis* - a work, action; Matthew 16
- Greek *poiema* - anything made, workmanship; Ephesians 2

BIBLIOGRAPHY

Artway.eu, http://www.artway.eu/content.php?id=796&lang=en&action=show

Baloche, Paul, *Open the Eyes of My Heart,* Integrity's Hosanna! Music (ASCAP) (adm at IntegratedRights.com), 1997. Song

Bell, Clive, *Art*, Capricorn Books, 1958. Print

Bonhoeffer, Dietrich, *The Cost of Discipleship,* Translated from the German NACH-FOLGE first published 1937 by Chr. Kaiser Verlag Muchen, by R.H. Fuller, with some revision by Irmgard Booth, first edition 1949, The Macmillian Company, 1963, 1967. Print

Booth, Eric, *The Everyday Work of Art: how artistic experience can transform your life*, Sourcebooks, Inc., 1997. Print

Britannica, com, https://www.britannica.com/art/organ-musical-instrument

Brewin, Kester, *Signs of Emergence: A Vision for Church That Is Organic/Net-worked/Decentralized/Bottom-up/Communal/Flexable/Always Evolving*, Baker Books, 2007. Print

Catholic Encyclopedia, https://www.catholic.org/encyclopedia/

ibid, Plain Chant; https://www.catholic.org/encyclopedia/view.php?id=9414

Chilvers, Ian, Osborne, Harold, and Farr, Dennis, ed., *The Oxford Dictionary of Art*, Oxford University Press, ©1994. Quote reproduced with permission of the Licensor through PLSclear. Print

Chujoy, Anatole, *The Dance Encyclopedia*, A.S. Barnes and Company, Inc., 1949. Print

Commins, Dorothy Berliner, *All about the Symphony Orchestra: and What it Plays*, Random House, Inc., 1961, Print

Couturier, M.-A., *Sacred Art*, texts selected by Dominique de Menil and Pie Duploye. Translation by Granger Ryan, University of Texas Press, Austin/the Menil Foundation. 1989. Print

De Mille, Agnes, *Portrait Gallery*, Houghton Mifflin Company, 1990. Print

Dewey, John, *Art As Experience*, Capricorn Books/G.P. Put-man and Sons, 1934, 1958. Print

Duke, Bill, *Sister Act 2: Back in the Habit*, 1993, Bill Duke, dir., James Orr, James Cruickshank, Judi Ann Mason, writers, Los Angeles, Touchstone Pictures. Film

Edwards, Betty, *Drawing on the Right Side of the Brain: A course in Enhancing Creativity and Artistic Confidence*, A Jeremy P. Tarcher/Putnam Books, 1989. Print

Fox, Matthew, *Creativity: where the divine and the human meet*, Jeremy P. Tarcher/Penguin, 2002, 2004. Print

Gibbs, Jr., William W., *Intentions in the Experience of Meaning*, Cambridge University Press, 1999. Print

Goldwalter, Robert, and Treves, Marco, ed., *Artist on Art, from the XIV to the XX Century*, Pantheon Books, 1972. Print

Greenburg, Clement, *The Collected Essays and Criticism, Perceptions and Judgments, 1939-1944, vol.1*, John O'Brian, ed., The University of Chicago Press, 1986. Print

Helmholtz, Hermann von, *On the Sensation of Tone: as a physiological basis for the theory of music*, Dover Publications, Inc., 1954. Print

Hine, Stuart K., *How Great Thou Art*, 1885. Song

Hughes, Robert, *The Mona Lisa Curse*, 2008; London, Oxford Film and Television for Channel 4, UK. Documentary

C. H, Kang and Ethel R. Nelson, *The Discovery of Genesis: How the Truths of Genesis Were Found Hidden in the Chinese Language*, Concordia Publishing, 1979. Print

Kavanaugh, Patrick, *The Spiritual Lives of Great Composers*, Sparrow Press, 1992. Print

Kulka, Tomas, *Kitsch and Art*, The Pennsylvania State University Press,: A Division of Pennsylvania State University Libraries and Scholarly Communications, 1996. Print

Lemmel, Helen Howarth (1863-1961), *Turn Your Eyes upon Jesus*, 1922. Song

Lynn, Steven, *Texts and Contexts: Writing About Literature with Critical Theory*, 3rd ed., Longman/Addison-Wesley Educational Publishers, 2001. Print

Mâle, Emile, *The Gothic Image: Religious Art in France of the Thirteenth Century*, trans. Dora Nussey, Harper and Row, Publishers, 1958, Icon Edition, 1972. Reproduced by permission of Taylor and Francis Group. Print

Mendelowitz, Daniel, *Drawing*, Holt, Rinehart, and Winston, Inc., 1967. Print

Merriam Webster.com, https://www.merriam-webster.com/dictionary/creativity

Montag, Warren, "What is at Stake in the Debate on Postmodernism," *Postmodernism and its Discontents: theories, practices*, ed. E. Ann Kaplan, Verso, 1988, 1990. Print

Nee, Watchman, *The Spiritual Man* (in Three Volumes), Volume One, Christian Fellowship Publishers, NY, 1968. Print

Plotinus, *The Enneads*, "1st Ennead, 6th Tractate: Beauty"; reproduced in *What is Art? Aesthetic Theory From Plato to Tolstoy*, ed. Alexander Sesonske, Oxford University Press, 1965. Print

Pope John Paul II, "*Letter of His Holiness Pope John Paul II to Artists*," Libreria Editrice Vaticana, 1999; www.vatican.va/content/john-paul-ii/en/letters/1999/documents/hf_jp-ii_let_23041999_artists.html. Html

Prince, Derek, *Thanksgiving, Praise and Worship, Incorporating Prayers and Proclamations*; Derek Prince Ministries—International/Word UK, 1991, 1993, 1999. Print

Reisner, Allen, *St. Louis Blues*, 1958, Allen Reisner, dir., Ted Sherdeman, Robert Smith, writers, Los Angeles, Paramount Pictures. Film

Richardson, Don, *Peace Child*, Regal Books, 1974, 2005. Print

Rookmaaker, H.R. *The Creative Gift: Essays on Art and the Creative Life*, Cornerstone Books, 1981. Print

Ross, Herbert, *Footloose*, 1984; Herbert Ross, dir., Dean Pritcher, writer; Los Angeles, Paramount Pictures, Phoenix Pictures, IndieProd Company Productions, Silver Screen Partners. Film

Routley, Erik, *The Church and Music: An Enquiry into the History, the Nature, and the Scope of Christian Judgment on Music*, Gerald Duckworth and Co. LTD., London, 1950, 1967. Print

Sanford, John and Paula, *The Elijah Task*, Victory House Inc., 1977. Print

Santayana, George, *The Sense of Beauty*, Dover Publications, 1896, 1955. Print

Schaefer, Francis, *Art and the Bible*, L'Abri Fellowship/Intervarsity Press, 1973. Print

Seashore, Carl, *Psychology of Music*, McGraw-Hill Book Company, Inc., 1938. Print

Sewall, Laura, *Sight and Sensibility: The Ecopsychology of Perception*, Jeremy P. Tarcher/Putnam, 1999. Print

Sheikh, Anees A. editor, *Imagery: Current Theory, Research, and Application*, John Wiley and Sons, Inc., 1983. Print

Siren, Oswald, *The Chinese on the Art of Painting*, Schocken Books, 1963. Print

Sorell, Walter, *Dance in Its Time: The Emergence of an Art Form*, Anchor Press/Double Day, 1981. Print

Sturken, Marita, Cartwright, Lisa, *Practices of Looking: An Introduction to Visual Culture*, Oxford University Press, 2001. Quotes reproduced with permission of the Licensor through PLSclear. Print

Taylor, Jill Bolte, PhD., *My Stoke of Insight*, Penguin Books, 2008. Print

Turkle, Sherry, *Life On The Screen: Identity in the Age of the Internet*, Touchstone/Simon and Schuster Inc., 1995. Print

Van Der Leeuw, Gerardus, *Sacred and Profane Beauty: The Holy in Art*, trans. David E. Green, Holt, Rinehart and Winston, Inc., 1961. Print

Vasari, Giorgio, *Lives of the Artists*, trans. George Bull, Penguin Books Ltd., 1965, 1982. Print

Wikipedia, https://en.wikipedia.org/wiki/All_Creatures_of_Our_God_and_King

, https://en.wikipedia.org/wiki/A_Mighty_Fortress_Is_Our_God

, https://en.wikipedia.org/wiki/Be_Thou_My_Vision

, https://en.wikipedia.org/wiki/Chapelle_du_Rosaire_de_Vence

, https://en.wikipedia.org/wiki/Marie-Alain_Couturier

, https://en.wikipedia.org/wiki/Notre_Dame_du_Haut

, https://en.wikipedia.org/wiki/%C3%89glise_Notre-Dame_de_Toute_Gr%C3%A2ce_du_Plateau_d%27Assy

, https://en.wikipedia.org/wiki/Phonograph

Wilson, Edwin, Goldfarb, Alvin, *Theater: The Lively Art, Fifth Edition*, McGraw-Hill Higher Education, McGraw Hill LLC, 1991, 2005. Print

von Oech, Roger, *A Whack on the Side of the Head: How You Can Be More Creative*, Creative Think, 1983, 1992. Print

BIBLIOGRAPHY

Velcro.com, https://www.velcro.com/original-thinking/our-story/
The Zondervan Pictorial Bible Dictionary, Merrill C. Tenney, general editor,
    Zondervan Publishing House, 1963, 1973. Print

ABOUT THE AUTHOR

Creativity led Rick to learn drawing and painting at a young age, beginning in middle school and high school. He pursued art in college and attended art school in Beverly, Massachusetts. He graduated from Monserrat College of Art with a Bachelor's degree in Fine Arts.

Rick grew up as a preacher's kid. He is familiar with the things that go on in churches, both good and bad. And he is familiar with the strengths and weaknesses of the art world.

He taught seminars on creativity, drawing, visual books with children, art's spiritual nature, and setting up church art programs. The subjects Rick taught, include drawing, painting, relief printmaking, graphic design, photography, clay, and 3-D work. He loves to teach, encouraging his students to pursue any art form that interests them.

Rick taught art classes in a private Christian school, and held classes for homeschooled students in middle school and high school. When he taught private classes to adults, he found the process often uncovered hidden fears that had been suppressed since childhood. He helped many adults let go of fears that were keeping them from releasing their God-given creativity.

Rick resides in Boise, Idaho with his wife, Jesika.